THE
CONCEPT OF AGGRESSION
IN INTERNATIONAL LAW

An SMU Law School Study

THE
CONCEPT OF AGGRESSION
IN INTERNATIONAL LAW

Ann Van Wynen Thomas
A. J. Thomas, Jr.

FOREWORD BY CHARLES O. GALVIN

SOUTHERN METHODIST UNIVERSITY PRESS • DALLAS

©1972 : SOUTHERN METHODIST UNIVERSITY PRESS : DALLAS

Library of Congress Catalog Card Number-72-86852
ISBN Number 0-87074-132-2

*The publication of this volume was made
possible through the generosity of*

ERIN BAIN JONES

TO

ERIN BAIN JONES

Author, Scholar, Philanthropist
and
Great Lady

~~~~~~~~~~~~~~~~~~~~~~~~

Ah! when shall all men's good
Be each man's rule, and universal Peace
Lie like a shaft of light across the land,
And like a lane of beams athwart the sea,
Thro' all the circle of the golden year?

Alfred, Lord Tennyson

CONTENTS

FOREWORD

THE ADMONITION of George Washington that this nation should avoid entangling alliances has often been quoted to support a position of detachment from the difficult problems of international relations. The course of history has not, however, permitted us such comfort. The technologies of travel and communication have made the world a small family, albeit of many diverse peoples, and the United States continually finds itself in the role of paterfamilias. The more we try to avoid involvement in other nations' affairs, so much the more do we become involved. And rightly so, for a great and powerful nation has the moral obligation to use its vast resources of materiel and personnel in world leadership.

To be effective, however, the United States in its spheres of influence must have an impact on the internal policies of enough nations to create a hegemony of peoples committed to freedom and justice. The distinction between exercising a subtle influence and an overt or covert intermeddling is difficult to define. Indeed, are such definitions even possible? The Thomases argue that they are and that they must be articulated:

> No serious student would contend today that aggression can be stopped simply because it is dispassionately and adequately defined. Nevertheless, definitions are one of the tools through which international behavior may be ameliorated. When the choices open to governments in the conduct of foreign relations are more or less clearly labeled as unlawful or lawful, greater consideration will be given to the ultimate choice made.

The historical search for definitions has been a tortuous one; the authors' account of it reflects those nagging anxieties which beset all men of good will who yearn for peace. What constitutes a provocation, what constitutes self-defense, what constitutes the subtle forms of direct and indirect aggression—all of these questions are part of the conceptual analysis which makes up the content of the definition. But the content is an ever expanding one as modern techniques make possible more sophisticated forms of aggression. Interventionary and subversive conduct against another state, propaganda harangues, fifth column activities, ideological coercion, and economic pressures are all part of an expanding content of the definition of aggression.

Definitions are, of course, useful to responsible nations. Whether or not they constitute a deterrent to the irresponsible is always an open question. Nevertheless, any effort toward precision in definition must be applauded as contributing another norm of conduct within the family of nations.

The Professors Thomas are extraordinarily well qualified to speak on this subject. Their experience in foreign service, numerous consultative commissions to agencies and offices of the Departments of State and Defense, and their distinguished record as scholars and teachers provide a wealth of background for this important work—a thoughtful, critical study containing historical and analytical discussion which will be of inestimable value to those who seek a greater understanding of international organizations, international conventions, and other arrangements.

As a long-time colleague and friend it is a personal privilege and honor for me to salute and congratulate them on the occasion of this latest publication which is another in a long series of impressive contributions to the literature in the fields of international law and international organizations.

CHARLES O. GALVIN

School of Law
Southern Methodist University
July, 1972

PREFACE

FOR MORE THAN HALF A CENTURY, statesmen, publicists, and internationalists have grappled with the concept of aggression. But all the days, weeks, and years spent upon this subject have not given birth to an internationally accepted definition. In this small volume we have traced the history of the concept, have highlighted the arguments surrounding it, and have concluded with our own views on that conduct which constitutes aggression. It is hoped that this synthesization will be of aid to the world's decision makers. In any event, it should apprise them of the *ad infinitum* and *ad nauseam* cycle of attempts to define, and we hope it will bring home to them the Shakespearean lament, "What fools these mortals be."

We wish to express our deep and sincere appreciation to Dean Charles O. Galvin, Dr. Cecil E. Johnson, and the Arnold Foundation for the encouragement extended in the writing and publication of this book. To Mrs. Nada Smit, the International Law Librarian at Underwood Law Library, we extend our heartfelt gratitude for her devoted attentiveness in obtaining all the necessary reference materials. As always our deepest obligation is to Mrs. Margaret Hartley, our editor, our friend, and our mentor who suffers with such gracious equanimity over the editing of our manuscripts.

ANN VAN WYNEN THOMAS
A. J. THOMAS, JR.

Dallas, Texas
July, 1972

THE
CONCEPT OF AGGRESSION
IN INTERNATIONAL LAW

CHAPTER ONE

INTRODUCTION

IN 1967, after almost ten years of neglect of the question, the United Nations once again turned its attention to the problem of determining the meaning of aggression in relation to present-day international circumstances. The General Assembly, in a resolution of December 18 of that year, after expressing the belief that a definition of aggression would be effective for the maintenance of international peace and for the taking of necessary measures for the prevention of aggression under the United Nations Charter, noted that no authoritative universal definition of the word existed. Thereupon it established a thirty-five-member Special Committee on the Question of Defining Aggression.[1]

That no commonly accepted definition of aggression is in being is surprising when one takes into account the multitude of studies and hours of debate which have been expended on the word since World War I.[2] Confusion is compounded by the highly conclusive and all-knowing manner in which the word is hurled in accusation by one state against another. In the Far East, the United States is charged by the Soviet Union with aggression in South Vietnam. The United States counters by placing the responsibility for the aggression in South Vietnam on the shoulders of North Vietnam and those other states which are acting in complicity with it.[3] In the Middle East, Israel is accused of aggression by the Arab states,[4] while Israel levels the same accusation against the Arabs.[5] In Latin America, Cuba cries aggression against her by the United States, the Organization of American States, and certain Latin American states. In turn these entities call Cuba's subversive acts against the hemisphere aggression.[6] The United States use of armed force in 1965 against the Dominican Republic was labeled aggression by some. This the United States denied, arguing to the contrary that in effect there took place an aggression against the Dominican Republic by the forces of international communism.[7] In Europe a series of aggressions are laid at the door of the Soviet Union, such as those directed against the Baltic States, Finland, Czechoslovakia, and Hungary. The Soviet Union refutes, and in turn complains of aggression by the "imperialist powers."[8]

These charges and countercharges would lend credence to the thought that one of the parties must be wrong in its accusations, or that the meaning of aggression carries differing connotations to different nations, or that propaganda hay is being made by loosely flinging the evil word "aggressor" against the opposition. Logically, therefore, a precise legal definition of aggression generally accepted by the international society would go far toward eliminating the confusion. The renewed efforts of the United Nations to reach a common agreement on the meaning of aggression should be universally welcomed. Nevertheless over the years strong and serious objection to the defining of aggression has been manifested, and this objection continues at the present time.

THE CASE AGAINST DEFINITION

Particularly in these recent and renewed discussions in the United Nations, some have taken exception to the attempt to define aggression, on the pragmatic and somewhat cynical ground of experience; a definition of aggression is, they say, simply unattainable. Those who support this point of view refer to the more than thirty years of effort which have failed to achieve a consensus as to its meaning. Further, they note that without a consensus of at least the major powers plus a large majority of the other members of the United Nations, a definition would be valueless.[9] As Professor Röling of the Netherlands points out, an exact and correct definition may be possible, but to have such a definition accepted by all or by a majority of the nations of the world or even by the greater portion of the authorities on international law "would be a remarkable and astonishing thing."[10] Some authorities would query Professor Röling's belief that an exact and correct or perfect definition may be possible, noting that a definition of aggression would have to be almost legally perfect, for if the definition were purely the result of compromise it would be of little assistance in determining in a specific case whether or not an act of aggression had been committed.[11]

Disapproval of continuing the search for a legal definition of aggression springs also from the fact that propagandists are often the ones most anxious to reduce the concept to a concise verbal formula, since they have an ulterior motive or an ax to grind and would be the ones to benefit from widespread acceptance of whatever definition they might favor at a particular moment.[12] "It may be significant that the definition of the aggressor peculiarly preoccupies the minds of those who are best prepared to commit aggression,"[13] wrote Professor John Bassett Moore just prior to World War II. Not only the definition itself, but also credit for the mere advancement of the notion to define and its discussion and study before international bodies are used as propaganda tools of expediency in the game of power politics.[14]

Some of the objection to a definition of aggression comes from common law oriented nations, for the common law legal technique proceeds on a cumulation of experience translated into viable legal norms, not on a basis of advance codification and prior definition of legal concepts.[15] It is argued that defining aggression would be defining in a vacuum. All of the elements which may be present in any particular case can never be known before the case arises. The existence of advanced definitions, whatever their nature, may be dangerous to the maintenance of international peace and security, for such definitions might make decisions of international organizations more or less automatic. This automatic stigmatization could be internationally injurious to an innocent nation—that is, one with a perfect legal defense. Or if a nation were truly an international delinquent, this prompt and automatic stigmatization might make the delinquent commit even more extensive crimes than it originally planned, on the theory that it might as well be hanged for a sheep as a lamb.[16] It is argued, therefore, that it is desirable to keep the term ambiguous, so that the international society can take ad hoc decisions resulting in an accumulation of case law on the issues which eventually will create guides to future activities and will permit the free development of the concepts along lines originally hoped for when the terminology was introduced into the law of nations. Professor Brierly has observed that progress toward a true international order should be sought not from a prolific growth of rules of general application—for that would be to assume a uniformity among states and their interests which often does not exist—but rather from the devising of particular solutions for particular problems as they arise. Therefore, he contended, it is wiser to continue to label certain actions as aggression on an ad hoc basis.[17]

It has also been claimed that with an established definition, a state desirous of committing acts of aggression would be pre-advised on how it might safely proceed to circumvent the letter of the definition.[18] A further objection to defining the term has been that most of the definitions generally suggested are purely legal in nature, minimizing the nonlegal elements. Since aggression involves elements of a political, military, economic, and social nature, purely legalistic definitions are condemned as inadequate. Of aggression it has been said that it "is a mixture of politics, economics, sociology and psychology but not much of jurisprudence. Thus aggression is like a chameleon; it changes its color circumstantially, . . . its contents, too, under different environments."[19]

It has been argued that progress in techniques of modern aggression create continuously new forms which cannot be foreseen and which, therefore, would mean that present-day definitions might soon be obsolete or at least incomplete.[20] Opponents of defining often revert to familiar features of constitutional law, showing that certain terms and phrases in many constitutional documents are left undefined mainly because it might be considered unwise to define them for all times. If an a priori definition is laid down, it is contended that it can freeze the ideas prevailing in a society at the time it is given and, since human society is anything but static, either it would be of little practical use or it might have the consequence of impeding change or progress, eventually leading to breaches of the definition and a consequent diminution of respect for international law.[21]

The question is further raised: who would be bound by the definition? Definitions set forth by international technicians, that is, authors, or students of international law, do not in any way bind nations or international organizations.[22] If an international body such as the Security Council of the United Nations should agree upon a definition, it would not bind the General Assembly, and vice versa.[23] Even if a majority of members in both bodies accepted the same definition, a question would arise as to whether it would be binding on nations opposed to its adoption.[24] Finally, it is pointed out that the failure of agreement on a definition is not and has not been the reason for the lack of peace in the world. The absence of peace is attributed to a failure of certain nations to live up to all of their obligations under the United Nations Charter, particularly those calling for a renunciation of the use of force.[25] Thus opponents of definitions intimate that "among the tasks vital for man's survival and welfare in a world of nuclear and interplanetary dimensions, the finding of an authoritative definition is among the least constructive."[26]

TYPES OF DEFINITIONS

Not only does opposition exist to defining at all, but there is no agreement as to the type of definition which might be adopted: enumerative, abstract, or mixed. The enumerative type lists the specific acts which are said to constitute aggression. This type has been subject to the criticism that it is not a real definition but merely an incomplete and rigid catalog of illegal acts. Inasmuch as this catalog of acts is divorced from the particular circumstances in which they occur and inasmuch as the acts are not judged in the light of all factors, legal and nonlegal, which precede them, an innocent state could automatically be considered guilty of an illegal act, while a guilty state would be exculpated. For example, some enumerative definitions state that the first declaration of war is an aggressive act and the nation declaring it is an aggressor. Under such a standard, Great Britain would be judged to have committed aggression upon Germany in 1939.[27]

Another problem is the fact that cases may have been omitted or forgotten in the definition and as a result certain nations might be encouraged to skirt the edges of legality by committing acts which have been over-looked. It has been pointed out[28] that it would be impossible to make an exhaustive listing of the criteria or subjects, and unless the listing was ex-haustive, an enumerative definition would be nearly useless for the purpose of deciding a concrete case. The enumerative approach, it is said, is based on the misconception that international law is a static and definable quantity and not subject to change as a result of the development of international relations.[29]

To overcome the criticisms of the enumerative definition, those who champion this type of approach would add the general statement that the acts listed are merely exemplaries of prohibited activities and are not in-tended to be exhaustive but are more in the nature of guidelines to be used by the appropriate international body in deciding whether or not a nation has committed an illegal act. For example, Article 9 of the Inter-American Treaty of Reciprocal Assistance (the Rio Treaty) lists a number of acts which are to be considered as aggression, but in addition it permits the Organ of Consultation to characterize other acts as such.[30]

In various international debates, it has become apparent that nations favoring the enumerative type of definition have done so because they see in this type a method for implementing goals which cannot be reached by regular means in international relations. Many enumerative advocates seek to place in the definition statements that certain particular international acts are always illegal regardless of the surrounding circumstances. Others have attempted to place in the definition statements that certain activities are never to be considered as aggression. In this latter context it has been sug-gested that the confiscation of foreign-owned property without prompt, adequate, or just compensation can never be called aggression no matter what the moral or legal rights of the injured nation, and, therefore, may never give rise to the right of self-defense, forceful or nonforceful, as a means of redress.[31]

The other two types, the abstract and the mixed, have also come in for their share of rebuke by those who think it is futile to attempt to distill these ideas into their purest essence.

The abstract type makes no attempt to specify particular acts but relies on a general formula which, opponents say, is often circulatory and generally indeterminate and is little improvement over a situation of no definition because it must rely on general words and phrases which themselves would require further definition. Professor Julius Stone points out that the affirm-ative plea in bar of self-defense against an accusation of aggression would require a definition of self-defense, which, under the United Nations Charter, must be spelled out in terms of aggression, and consequently would merely bring the matter back to what constitutes aggression.[32]

It is intimated that abstract definitions permit criminal nations to engage in long and dangerous debates about the nature of their acts on the basis that since there are no clear and unequivocal definitions, whatever acts they engaged in cannot be considered illegal because there can be no criminality without a definite crime.[33]

The mixed type of definition makes use of an abstract formula and then lists a number of particular acts by way of example. Its opponents claim that this has the disadvantages of both the enumerative and the general definition. A variation of the mixed type is the inclusion, at the end, of a closing statement which leaves the final determination as to whether a concrete case falls within the definition up to the decision of an international agency. It is complained that this returns the whole problem to the present situation, where each case brought to the attention of the United Nations is judged today by that body without recourse to definitions.[34]

THE CASE FOR DEFINITIONS

To those who believe that explicit formulation of definitions is instrumental to all legal inquiry, the arguments against defining aggression are largely nonsensical. If law is a science, it is said, then scientific techniques must be used and among these techniques is the never-ending search for accurate definitions of legal concepts. Even though there are difficulties in defining the term, this is no excuse for saying the task is hopeless.[35] As Professors M. McDougal and F. Feliciano declare:

It is of course as futile to seek a reificatory, absolutist, and all-sufficing definition of aggression as of any other legal concept or word. But the impossibility of absolute precision does not necessarily render complete confusion desirable. In this most fundamental problem of all, as in lesser problems, legal principles might be formulated which would serve the same functions that other legal principles serve—that of bringing to the focus of attention of a decision-maker relevant factors in context which should rationally affect decision. From this perspective, the basic task is one of categorizing such variable contextual factors with respect to the distinction between permissible and non-permissible coercion.[36]

Another strong advocate of definition is Professor Sohn, who points out that the simple fact that the Soviet Union has been a leading advocate of definition, seeing therein an advancement of the interests of international communism, does not mean that definitions are evil per se. Sohn points out that many of the smaller and newer nations have also indicated interest in finding definitions for aggression, particularly in some of its newer manifestations such as indirect aggression, economic aggression, and ideological aggression, because they have a basic fear of these activities by more powerful nations and wish to spell out in the greatest possible detail the circumstances in which the United Nations should legally come to their assistance.[37] The failure of the western nations to come forth with adequate definitions has resulted in, among other things, a psychological propaganda defeat for the West, because the Soviets have said that the western powers must have designs against the political and economic integrity of the developing nations of Asia, Africa, and Latin America,[38] or else they would not oppose defining.

To the argument that all definitions would be worthless unless unanimously accepted by the great powers, the intermediate powers and the small powers, Sohn replies that to be effective a definition need not be adopted by an overwhelming majority, let alone unanimously by all the nations of the world. He points out that the Uniting for Peace Resolutions of the General Assembly, even if opposed to the wishes of a great power, have still operated most effectively in some cases.[39]

Those who favor the enumerative type of definition declare that it has the advantage of setting forth the elements which constitute a crime, indicating without ambiguity the type of acts which will give rise to a charge of aggression, and will be of aid to the victim state because it will know that it has an unquestionable right to take action against such illicit actions either by bringing the issue before an international body or by employing the inherent right of self-defense. Preestablished laws describing illicit acts are juridically preferable to leaving the problem to be decided in each individual case according to particular circumstances. In the latter instance many extraneous elements may enter into the consideration of the problem. Without definition international bodies, rather than settle the issue according to law, are more apt to compromise, conciliate, and arbitrate even clear-cut issues of illegality. The more automatic a definition is, the more likely the injured party will be to obtain justice according to law.[40]

Those like Dr. Alfaro who feel that abstract definitions are better than enumerative definitions point out that it is impossible in a world that changes continuously for the human mind to foresee all the cases, forms, manners, eventualities, and circumstances that may be present in any given future fact situation.[41] Therefore, it is always probable that the enumerations of prohibited or punishable acts would be incomplete and some loophole would be left through which a wrongdoer could escape with impunity. Nevertheless, advocates of the enumerative definition note that the fact that a wrongdoer may find a loophole and engage in activities which are not expressly prohibited yet which should have been prohibited is not a situation peculiar to the field of international law. The problem is common to most fields of law and calls for continued efforts to develop the law to decrease the possibilities of evasion of the statutory rule whenever one encounters such means of escape. Although this may bring about a patchwork of plugged-up loopholes, still there is no valid reason to abolish a rule entirely just because some offender has succeeded in escaping the law with impunity.

Some jurists favor the abstract type of definition because this avoids the danger of imprecision, of patchwork, and at the same time avoids the danger of excessive rigidity. The fact that the terms used in abstract definitions might themselves be in need of further definition merely indicates that the law is undergoing a process of sophistication, which is typical of any system of law. All civilized legal order progresses from general prohibitions of acts violating the interests of other persons to more precisely defined specifics.[42]

In answer to the contention that in constitutional law certain terminology is purposely left undefined so that later generations will not become entrapped in an unchanging formula of words, it is replied that words now thought to be nebulous were not considered unclear when placed in the constitution.

Those favoring definition also point out that in the absence of definition each side is completely free to determine what is or is not an aggressive act. Any agreed-upon definition is therefore better than none. If one believes at all in attempts to maintain international peace, the choice should not be between defining and not defining, but rather where to draw the line as to what is permitted and what is forbidden.[43]

To the argument that if a definition were possible, it would have already been found either by the League of Nations or the United Nations, the answer has been given that either of these groups could long since have come up with definitions had they not sought to have the decisions adopted unanimously.[44] As most delegates to these bodies represent governments with distinct ideologies, they must abide by the instructions they receive. Some authorities maintain that a nonofficial definition would be best. It should not be impossible for a group of scholars to sit down, rid their minds of national bias, and derive a definition which would be dispassionate and juridical. It would then not matter whether or not the nations of the world accepted such definitions, for they would be used as a scholarly yardstick, not as another new propaganda technique.[45]

It has been indicated that the ideas of aggression are "natural notions" which need not be defined because they are known by intuition.[46] To this the reply is made that if people were all in the same stage of civilization and if all mankind had the same intuitions as to what is lawful or unlawful, what is good or what is bad, the earth would be paradise. Unfortunately this is not yet true, and one only adds to international anarchy by stating that legal definitions would be artificial constructions rather than natural notions.[47] As Kelsen so aptly points out, definitions are important, but even with a definition one may still be faced with the problem of its difficulty in application to a concrete set of facts.[48]

Although some enthusiasts for definition see in a universally accepted verbal formula the panacea which is capable of guaranteeing the maintenance of world peace, most advocates are more realistic in their attitudes. A definition is not automatically regarded as a magic formula which will wave away all the world's ills. It is simply recognized that if a definition is available, in certain types of cases, and in certain instances, the potential aggressor will think twice before disrupting international relations. In this sense, a definition would hang over the head of a potential wrongdoer like the sword of Damocles. Nations are less apt to take certain steps if they know that such steps will instantaneously and automatically label them in the eyes of the world as the wrong-doer. Without accurate legal definitions, defenses can be set up for excuse, which will merely add confusion to an already confused issue. With a definite verbal formula, such diversionary techniques become more difficult.

All collective security systems are directly related to the notion of aggression, so it would seem logically impossible to have an adequate system of collective security claiming to be juridical in nature in the absence of definite norms relating to the act of aggression.[49] This can clearly be seen from the many debates over the issue whether or not the concept of aggression includes indirect aggression. If no one is sure, no state can be completely sure of its legal rights and duties under a collective security arrangement.

World War II, it is said, highlighted the danger of having undefined concepts cluttering up legal documents such as treaties. Had there been at that time a definition of the term aggression, and if it had been accepted by the major powers, certain nations might have faced international disapprobation much sooner in their aggressive careers, and this might well have changed the course of history.[50]

It has been claimed that because the international atmosphere is full of suspicion and hate, now is not the auspicious time to define the term. On the other hand, when all is peaceful and harmonious, there is no great urgency to define and it goes undefined. Actually there is never a right time to define, but this does not mean that the term should be used without definition.

Definitions do not poison the atmosphere between nations as much as does lack of definition.

THE CHOICE

The present confused state of affairs with relation to the definition of aggression is scarcely satisfactory. There is no agreement on whether or not definitions are necessary, and if necessary what they should include. The failure of various groups to formulate an acceptable definition indicates that the task is difficult, but this does not mean that it is unnecessary or impossible.

True, international law has often been called a primitive system of law; but if it is to be regarded as a legal system at all, it must consist of legal norms which can be referred to when certain fact situations arise. All members of a legal order have a legitimate right to know in advance what conduct the order prohibits. A legal order which leaves its subjects in complete uncertainty about the content of their obligations cannot be called even a primitive legal order.[51] As long as aggression is not legally defined it must remain a predominantly political concept. Nevertheless, international treaties have given to certain international organs powers of decision over questions involving this principle—powers of decisions which have legal consequences for the whole society of states. Therefore it is imperative that the concept be taken out of the political arena and placed into juridical focus; and this can be done only by defining the legal nature of the act. Definitions, of course, in and of themselves, have no effect. The effect arises from the application of a legal rule attaching a sanction to an act which, in accordance with the definition contained in the rule, has been declared by the law-applying agency to be illegal.

Unquestionably there will be inherent shortcomings in any definition that might be proposed. This has led many an authority to believe that the only sensible way to deal with problems of aggression is "to play it by ear," to leave it up to an appropriate international body to determine in each individual case whether or not aggression has taken place.

But how would such a body arrive at a decision? Statesmen involved must have some standards to which they refer, consciously or unconsciously, so in effect they are defining the issues; but they are defining them in moments of tension and crisis. It is correct to assume that they must have some criteria of reference, since otherwise any determination would be so arbitrary that it would neither merit international respect nor obtain international acceptance. The choice then is not between definition and no definition but between relatively informed, sophisticated, and objective theoretical propositions which have been carefully formulated in the course of professional analysis, and a definition which may be based on theoretical generalizations, but, because it emerges under hit-or-miss circumstances at a time when passions are running high, is full of dangerous pitfalls of which the statesmen may be aware but which they cannot avoid because of the particular fact situation which requires immediate solution.

No serious student would contend today that aggression can be stopped simply because it is dispassionately and adequately defined. Nevertheless, definitions are one of the tools through which international behavior may be ameliorated. When the choices open to governments in the conduct of foreign relations are more or less clearly labeled as unlawful or lawful, greater consideration will be given to the ultimate choice made.

CHAPTER TWO

THE SEARCH FOR DEFINITIONS

EARLY MEANINGS

ONLY SINCE World War I has aggression become a term of controversy subject to examination by jurists.[1] But prior to that time various meanings were attributed which still cluster around the modern concept. The first contribution of Latin consisted of the idea of starting or committing the first act. This was derived from the verb *aggredior*, meaning to go to, to approach some one with any purpose, even a peaceful purpose. A later Latin use conceived it in terms of nonpeaceful approaches. Here its meaning was thought of as to go against one in a hostile manner, to fall on, to attack, to assault.[2] Both of these elements, the idea of the first act as well as of violence or force, have been carried down to modern times, so that aggression is often defined today as a first hostile act. These Latin definitions were directed to an act committed by an individual person or group and had no reference to relations among states. Until the nineteenth century aggression was, for the most part, although not exclusively, used in a private criminal law sense, indicating an attack made by one person upon another without due cause, giving to the attacked the right to use force to protect himself. Consequently self-defense became a correlative of aggression. When the term became common in international legal circles, this connection was retained.[3]

The word *aggression* came also to be used in two senses—legitimate and illegitimate aggression. Legitimate aggression was that committed by some authority making use of its power to punish and prevent crime or misconduct. Illegal aggression was that committed without justification, as for an example, an illegal attack by one private individual against another. This distinction was accepted as late as 1937 by such an outstanding internationalist as the Cuban jurist Bustamante, who was of the belief that it was important to specify whether the aggression was lawful or unlawful.[4] Today it is generally admitted that to talk of legitimate or illegitimate aggression in the relations between or among states is erroneous. Aggression is considered to be a word carrying the connotation of illegality in and of itself.[5] Nevertheless, Bustamante based his reasoning on a famous authority. Suarez, an early Spanish classicist in the field of international law, spoke, in the seventeenth century, of aggressive war as something moral and legal.[6] Aggressive war, as he defined it, consisted of war instituted for redress against an injustice already consummated. He went on to say that such a war may be both right and necessary.

The Swiss publicist Vattel, on the other hand, writing a century later, could not agree with Suarez. In more modern parlance and in speaking of a state's right to employ force or make war against another state, he declared: "Now if anyone attacks a nation or violates her perfect rights, he does her injury. Then and not till then that nation has a right to repel an aggressor and reduce him to reason."[7] Here an aggressor becomes a violator of rights—a wrongdoer. Aggression was regarded as delictual.

Treaties of defensive alliance concluded during the nineteenth century often obligated the contracting parties in case any one of them were attacked to consider themselves all attacked in order to repel the aggression. Aggression was equated with military attack by the armed forces of one state against another. In a technical military sense the word was a neutral one signifying a first attack. An aggressor was one who committed a first attack or a first act of hostility; therefore, *any* first attack might constitute an aggression obligating other contracting states of the defensive alliance to come to the assistance of any state attacked who was also a contracting party. It is doubtful if these treaties were understood in such an expansive sense. Interpretations of such treaties demonstrate that the word "aggression" as used therein meant an armed attack of great magnitude; i.e., there was a close connection between such an aggression and war. Furthermore, the attack to invoke the terms of the treaty had to be an unprovoked attack or aggression and of such large proportion as to bring about a situation necessitating self-defense on the part of the state attacked or subjected to the aggression. Aggression thus came to be identified with aggressive war, bearing a connotation of illegality, for an aggression or aggressive war instituted against a state permitted that state to react with a right—a legal right—of self-defense. This being true, it followed that an act of aggression against which a legal right of self-defense is recognized must itself be something more than a neutral concept. It must be considered as a wrong, an illegality.[8]

These mid-nineteenth-century ideas of aggression still reflected the concepts of the just and unjust war of the canonists of the Middle Ages. However, with the arrival of the modern age of positivism, which greatly influenced international legal thinking, it became specious to speak of a legal right of self-defense guaranteed by positive law or to speak of an illegal war of aggression. War and resort to war were recognized as political fact only. Aggressive war might be considered as an unjust war, but this was only a moral, as distinguished from a legal, concept. In positive international law it was admitted that every state had as an attribute of sovereignty the right to make war.[9] It was free to pursue its aims by recourse to force unrestrained by law. But the arrival of the mass army, as well as the continuing discovery of ever more effective weapons, led to some serious rethinking about the limitations on the rights of nations to resort to war which sought to reestablish aggressive war as an illegal enterprise.

THE LEAGUE OF NATIONS PERIOD

At the end of World War I new attempts were made to limit or abolish the right of states to resort to force of arms. Reactions against the carnage of this war engendered the notion that aggressive war at least should be made illicit. The Treaty of Versailles led the way by naming Germany as an aggressor and by making her responsible for losses suffered as a result of her aggression.[10] Aggressive war was not outlawed as a crime, but this action against Germany indicated a crystallization of opinion that a state starting a war by attacking first must be penalized.[11]

After 1919 and the appearance of the League of Nations the notion of aggressive war became of real significance in international law. The concept of aggression was introduced into positive international law by the Covenant of the League and became tied in with the collective security system of the international community. The Covenant made war or threat thereof a matter of concern for the League, which was called upon to take action deemed wise and effectual to safeguard the peace of nations.[12] Article 10 placed upon the members the obligation to respect and preserve against *external aggression* the territorial integrity and existing political independence of all League members. The Council was called upon to advise upon the means by which this obligation was to be fulfilled in case of any threat or danger of such aggression. It will be noted that aggression as used in Article 10 was nowhere defined in the Covenant. Aggression and aggressive war would appear to be implicitly prohibited by Article 10, but resort to war was not completely outlawed. It was outlawed only in case certain preestablished proceedings seeking peace proved useless. Article 12 in effect established two types of war: lawful and unlawful. It provided:

The members of the League agree that if there should arise between them any dispute likely to lead to a rupture, they will submit the matter either to arbitration or judicial settlement or to inquiry by the Council, and they agree in no case to resort to war until three months after the award by the arbitration or the judicial decision, or the report by the Council.

On the face of it a war would be lawful if begun three months after award or judicial decision or report, but unlawful before. Actually such a provision did not establish a prohibition of war but was in fact a moratorium. War became licit after certain dilatory proceedings ended.

The Covenant did not abolish war. It distinguished between different wars, but not on the classic doctrine of just or unjust war. The illegality of resort to war was a function not of the intrinsic injustice of the cause of war, but of the breach of a formal procedural requirement. This meant that if a state failed to fulfill these requirements, even though it had a perfectly just reason to go to war, it could be declared guilty of resort to illegal war, while a state which complied with these requirements without a just cause for war would be acting legally. The Covenant attempted to replace the idea of war by an interdiction against aggression. But the failure of the Covenant to define aggression and the fact that it did not absolutely prohibit resort to war were soon recognized to be dangerous gaps in the system of collective security.[13] Article 10 became the subject of study and discussion, and the long, unending attempt to define aggression began.

In 1923 the Third Commission of the Assembly of the League of Nations transmitted to member governments the draft of a Treaty of Mutual Assistance[14] which attempted to identify wars of aggression as an international crime. The treaty was accompanied by a commentary relative to a definition of the term "aggression,"[15] which admitted that in view of conditions of modern warfare, no universally acceptable definition could be agreed upon by the members. The proposed treaty of mutual assistance was abandoned in 1924 because of prevailing thought that without a definition of aggression assurances of collective defenses against aggression were useless.[16] Equally abortive was the Geneva Protocol, signed in 1924,[17] which in its preamble again declared aggression to be an international crime. Article 2 prohibited war unless fought to resist aggression or in accord with decisions of the League under the Covenant. Aggression was circuitously defined in Article 10 as resort to war in violation of the League Covenant or the Protocol.

The Treaty of Locarno, concluded in 1925, prohibited resort to war. Excepted therefrom, however, were war or force used in the exercise of the right of self-defense; force recognized as legitimate by the League of Nations Covenant; and forceful action taken against a flagrant violation of Articles 42 and 43 of the Versailles Treaty which demilitarized the left bank of the Rhine and the breach of which was declared to constitute an act of aggression. In 1927, the Assembly of the League passed a resolution under which all wars of aggression were said to be prohibited; nations were to resort only to pacific means to settle their international disputes. And in 1928 the Sixth Pan-American Conference adopted a resolution asserting that a "war of aggression constitutes a crime against the human species . . . all aggression is illicit and . . . prohibited."[18]

Another major effort to make aggressive war illicit took place in 1928 in Paris at the signing of the General Treaty for the Renunciation of War, more commonly called the Kellogg Briand Pact or the Pact of Paris.[19] The signatories to the treaty agreed to renounce war both as a tool of self-help to right international wrongs and as an act of national sovereignty to change existing rights. Under its terms war was apparently still permitted in cases of legitimate self-defense and as an instrument of collective action to restrain an aggressor, although the word aggressor was neither mentioned nor defined.

The Soviet Union had not been invited to participate in the negotiations which led to the Kellogg-Briand Pact, but eventually it did sign the treaty. Nevertheless, in a note to the French ambassador in Moscow, Mr. Litvinov commented upon "the indefiniteness and obscurity" in the formulation of the "prohibition of war," which permitted various interpretations. What was needed was a clear definition of aggression plus a general, complete, and immediate disarmament of all nations. For not only, it was stated, should all international wars be forbidden, but also all wars attempting to restrain national movements of liberation as well as interventions, blockades, military occupation of foreign territory and foreign ports, and severances of diplomatic relations.[20]

It was at about this time that the phrase "indirect aggression" made its debut in international legal terminology. The French, thinking in terms of their historic enemy, Germany, sought guarantees from other nations to ward off the danger of German invasion which was referred to as *agression directe*. But France was not content with guarantees against direct attack only. She believed that such guarantees would not stand the test if Germany were allowed to gain mastery over Central and Eastern Europe. She therefore spoke of a second type of threat to security, which she called *agression indirecte*, which would consist of an attack by Germany on one or more of France's eastern or southeastern neighbors. France sought measures to prevent this contingency.[21]

Indirect aggression covered a wide realm of possibilities which France had little desire to define or delimit with precision. Any effort to change the status quo in the east or southeast of Europe would render France less secure and might even threaten her with invasion in the more or less remote future. Since the German military machine was beginning to redevelop, this French concept of indirect aggression became more important, involving the whole controversial issue of the territorial, economic, and national problems of Central and Eastern Europe.

In 1933 aggression and its definition were subjected to much consideration in the context of disarmament at the Conference for the Reduction and Limitation of Armaments. Mr. Litvinov, of the Soviet Union, presented a detailed definition of aggression by listing specifically acts considered to be such. According to the Soviet proposal an aggressor would be the first to commit actions such as a declaration of war upon another state, invasion of the territory of another state with or without a declaration of war, an attack made on the territory, vessels or aircraft of another state, and naval blockade. The Soviet project was sent to the Committee on Security Questions of the conference.[22] The committee introduced certain amendments to the proposal, the most important being the addition of a fifth act of aggression:

5. Provision of support to armed bands formed in its territory which have invaded the territory of another State, or refusal, notwithstanding the request of the invaded State, to take in its own territory all the measures in its power to deprive those bands of all assistance or protection.[23]

This added provision defines that which is now often described as indirect aggression, i.e., those cases in which a state without admitting any responsibility in the hostilities deriving therefrom encourages, permits, or tolerates armed groups of foreigners or nationals to take armed actions against another state. All the acts of aggression, including this provision relating to indirect aggression, became Article 1 in the text of the "Act Relating to the Definition of the Aggressor." Article 2 then went on to state that political, military, economic, or other considerations could not serve as justification for the acts of aggression set forth in Article 1, and Article 3 made the "Act Relating to the Definition of the Aggressor" an integral part of the General Convention for the Reduction and Limitation of Armaments.[24]

This enumeration of the acts of aggression by the Committee on Security Questions was the most detailed which had as yet appeared. It went far beyond the then accepted notion of aggressive war. This enumerative type of definition was undoubtedly rigid, and it permitted very little room for maneuvering in international bodies which might be called upon to interpret it. It became a provisional part of the Draft Disarmament Convention of 1933, and was a model for a number of later nonaggression treaties between the Soviet Union and certain other nations: Afghanistan, Estonia, Latvia, Lithuania, Persia, Poland, Rumania, and Turkey.[25] Finland acceded at a later time.[26] It is an interesting aside to note that among these nations signing the treaties of nonaggression with the Soviet Union, only Afghanistan, Persia,

Turkey, and part of Finland remain free nations outside the Soviet orbit. From this evidence, it can be said that whatever the technical merits of the Soviet definition, it did not act as a mighty legal barrier to acts of aggression, direct or indirect.

The League of Nations efforts to define conduct deemed to be aggressive sputtered to a halt as the majority of member nations no longer deemed such a definition to be of critical importance. It was assumed that the juridical conscience of the international community would instinctively perceive aggression when it occurred and would react against it. But in 1931, when Japan invaded Manchuria, although the Assembly recognized that the military actions of Japan could not be regarded as measures of self defense, it still would not go so far as to brand Japan as an aggressor.[27] In connection with the Chaco War between Bolivia and Paraguay in 1934, the League took the position that as each party claimed ownership of the Chaco and therefore maintained that it was waging defensive war in its own territory, there could be no legal determination of who was the aggressor.[28]

Although finding Italy guilty of violating the Covenant of the League in the Italo-Ethiopian dispute of 1935, the Council of the League found this violation to be a breach of Article 12, the article requiring a three month cooling-off period, not a breach of Article 10, which would have forced the labeling of Italy's actions as aggression.[29]

Only in the case of the Russian invasion of Finland in 1939 was the juridical conscience of the League finally able unequivocally to recognize that an aggression had taken place.[30]

The League of Nations sought to define aggression as part of a scheme of collective security, but at the 1945 London Conference the meaning of aggression became of import for a different purpose. Here France, the Soviet Union, the United States, and the United Kingdom agreed to set up an International Military Tribunal to try certain individuals for the crime of "aggressive war-making."[31] The United States proposed that the Charter of the International Military Tribunal should contain a definition much along the lines of the definition of 1933.[32] The Soviet Union took the stand that for this purpose it was unalterably opposed to the inclusion of a definition of *aggression* or *aggressor* in the tribunal charter,[33] and consequently the United States proposal was rejected. The indictments against the war criminals simply charged that the individuals were guilty of planning, preparing, and initiating aggressive war. Not only was the Nuremberg Tribunal not given a definition of aggression, but it did not itself formulate such a definition.[34] From a review of historical events it was able to find that the defendants had planned and waged aggressive war.

The League of Nations failed in its quest for a definition of aggression as a means to prevent nations from taking actions which would endanger world peace and collective security. The Nuremberg Tribunal punished individuals for participating in the crimes which were thought to be encompassed in the broad idea of international aggression without a definition of aggression.

THE UNITED NATIONS ERA

San Francisco

Just prior to the close of World War II, the question of the definition of aggression for purposes of international peace and security arose again at the Dumbarton Oaks Conference, but no action was taken. When the nations met at San Francisco to draft the United Nations Charter, two proposed definitions were offered, one by Bolivia and the other by the Philippines.

The Bolivian definition set forth acts to be regarded as aggression similar to those contained in the 1933 "Act Relating to the Definition of the Aggressor"; but certain additional acts were submitted, such as intervention, refusal to submit the causes of a dispute to peaceful means provided for its settlement, and refusal to comply with a judicial decision of an international court.[35]

The Philippine definition would designate a nation as an aggressor if it should be the first party to commit acts such as a declaration of war, invasion or attack against the territory, public vessel, or aircraft of another nation, blockade, and finally

[t]o interfere with the internal affairs of another nation by supplying arms, ammunition, money or other forms of aid to any armed band, faction or group, or by establishing agencies in that nation to conduct propaganda subversive of the institutions of that nation.[36]

Here was a broader condemnation of support to armed bands than had been advanced previously, for the definition also included subversive propaganda as aggression, although propaganda emanating from agencies established in the suspected aggressor's own territory would be excluded.

The conference ruled against the inclusion of any definition in the Charter,[37] leaving the new organization, through the Security Council, the right to decide without prior restraint when a "threat or use of force" or a "threat to the peace, breach of the peace or act of aggression" occurred.

The United Nations Charter

The undefined term *aggression* is used in the United Nations Charter as an act along with threats to and breaches of the peace which should necessitate collective coercive measures to maintain or restore international peace and security.[38] Members are forbidden to use force against the territorial integrity or political independence of any state or in any manner inconsistent with the purposes of the United Nations.[39] Excepted from this interdiction is the use of force in the exercise of individual or collective self-defense[40] or in the participation in United Nations collective measures to enforce and maintain international peace.[41]

During the League of Nations era the primary emphasis was placed on attempting to find a definition which would distinguish illegal aggressive war from legal defensive war. The United Nations Charter deleted the term "war" altogether, substituting "threat or use of force," "threat to the peace," "breach of the peace," and "act of aggression." These expressions cover a wide range of gradations of intensity of coercion including not only force but also all applications of coercion of a lesser intensity or magnitude. Thus the word "war" has been replaced by more comprehensive terms which can cover many hostile activities, whether regular armies or armed bands are involved, whatever the weapons used, and whether committed openly or otherwise. This approach, which would seem to include the use of overt and covert force, might have been useful if greater clarification had been given in the charter. This was not done. And because the framers of the charter deliberately chose comprehensive words without defining them, the debate of defining magic words was to continue.

In November, 1950, the First Committee of the General Assembly of the United Nations was considering the question of "Duties of States in the Event of the Outbreak of Hostilities" when Yugoslavia, uneasy at the intensification of Soviet pressure on its northeastern frontiers, offered a resolution calling upon every state concerned in any outbreak of hostilities to proclaim its readiness to issue a cease fire and withdrawal order within forty-eight hours. Any state failing to comply would be designated an aggressor.[42]

The position immediately taken by the Soviet Union was that it would be necessary to define aggression before thus prescribing the duties of states.[43] A Soviet resolution was thereupon introduced which submitted for adoption the substance of its enumerated draft resolution on the definition of aggression of 1933, except that this resolution omitted any reference to the support of armed bands.[44] This was called to the Soviet Union's attention by certain delegations.[45]

Yugoslavia amended its proposal to provide that states in armed conflict should take all steps compatible with self-defense to bring the conflict to an early end and should proclaim their readiness within twenty-four hours to discontinue military operations and to withdraw all military forces on terms agreed upon by the parties or indicated by the appropriate organ of the United Nations.[46] This and another draft resolution which would have the International Law Commission consider the definition of aggression were submitted to the General Assembly. That body determined that the issue of defining aggression should be sent to the International Law Commission for study.

Before this body could begin its work, the U.S.S.R. requested the General Assembly to include on the agenda for the Fifth Session the item entitled "Declaration on the Removal of the Threat of a New War and the Strengthening of Peace and Security among the Nations." The Assembly approved and submitted the matter to the First Committee for consideration and report.[47] A draft resolution having an important relationship to aggression was adopted by the First Committee, which recommended it to the General Assembly where it was also adopted.[48] The resolution, known as the "Peace Through Deeds Resolution,"[49] dealt in part with international aggression. The General Assembly condemned "the intervention of a State in the internal affairs of another State for the purpose of changing its legally established government by the threat or use of force," and reaffirmed that "whatever the weapons used, any aggression, whether committed openly, or by fomenting civil strife in the interests of a foreign power, or otherwise, is the gravest of all crimes against peace and security throughout the world."[50]

In this resolution not only was open aggression branded as criminal activity but the "fomenting of civil strife in the interest of a foreign power" was also included as illegal aggression; and the phrase, "or otherwise" implied that aggression might take place when armed force is neither used nor immediately threatened.

The International Law Commission and the Draft Code of Offenses Against the Peace and Security of Mankind

In 1947 the General Assembly of the United Nations directed the International Law Commission to formulate the principles of international law which had been recognized by the Nuremberg Trial and to prepare a Draft Code of Offenses Against the Peace and Security of Mankind.[51] By 1951 a draft code had been adopted by the Commission which was submitted to the General Assembly.[52] The offenses listed in the draft were stated to be crimes under international law for which the responsible individuals were to be punished. Any act of aggression was declared criminal. Again aggression was not actually defined, although the employment by the authorities of a state of armed force against another state (other than armed force used in self-defense or in pursuance of a decision or recommendation by a competent organ of the United Nations) was included within the meaning of aggression.[53] Threats to resort to an aggression by the authorities of a state were also described as offenses against the peace and security of mankind.[54] Acts which were often called indirect aggression, such as the undertaking or encouragement of activities calculated to foment civil strife or terrorist activities in another state,[55] were listed as offenses, although no label of aggression indirect or otherwise was put upon them.

The General Assembly, rather than adopting or rejecting the proposed code, merely sent it on to member states for their comments and observations, which were to be taken up by the following year by the International Law Commission.[56] From the standpoint of those seeking a definition of aggression, the code was deficient. It did not list acts deemed to be aggression other than the illegal use of armed force. Under the draft code every act of aggression was considered a crime, but no attempt was made to enumerate acts of aggression exhaustively. The employment of armed force was definitely called aggression. Aggression could apparently be committed by other acts, but what these other acts might be was left open.

During the second study of the International Law Commission on the draft code, some discussion was focused on the possibility and utility of defining aggression in the code; but first the problem of the threat of aggression as a crime was considered. Several members suggested that it was difficult to characterize a threat of aggression as a prospective crime. For example, Dr. Ricardo Alfaro of Panama noted that in 1947 and 1948 Cuba had accused the United States of economic aggression in raising its import duty on Cuban sugar, and wondered whether a mere threat to take such a measure could be considered an international crime.[57] The French representative thought that a threat could be an aggressive act "if it was a serious threat, not merely pressure," but he would leave it up to a judge to decide the nuance[58] It was generally agreed that a serious threat to use armed force would certainly be illegal, and consequently this should be retained in the draft code.[59]

At the same meeting, the problem of incursion by armed bands was raised. Mexico stressed the point that if the members of the band were revolutionary nationals of the invaded state, they could not be considered criminals although officials of the state from which or through which they passed might be internationally responsible.[60] Others believed that even the members should be made individually responsible. The Colombian representative proposed to include, as a crime, "all forms of propaganda . . . intended or calculated to cause or encourage any threat to peace. . . ." He suggested that Streicher was convicted at Nuremberg primarily because of his propaganda against peace. Others opposed this as too vague, unmanageable, and apt to create "freedom of speech" problems. The suggestion was withdrawn.[61]

When the commission turned to the problem of defining aggression, in accord with the Soviet request and the General Assembly resolution,[62] it was again faced with the fact that most of its members were of the opinion that aggression could not be usefully defined. However, a number of members believed otherwise, and therefore the Commission worked for several sessions over a draft definition of aggression. The draft read:

Aggression is the threat or use of force by a State or Government against another State, in any manner, whatever the weapons used and whether openly or otherwise, for any purpose other than individual or collective self-defense or in pursuance of a decision or recommendation by a competent organ of the United Nations.[63]

But when it came to a vote the commission refused to adopt this definition.[64]

In 1954 the International Law Commission had before it a revised version of a text for a Draft Code of Offenses against the Peace and Security of Mankind which had been changed in the light of comments received from governments. Any act of aggression, which again was undefined but was said to include the use of armed force by one state against another except in self-defense or in pursuance of a proper United Nations order, was declared an offense, as was a threat to resort to an act of aggression. Not called aggression, but listed as offenses were the preparation for the employment of armed force against a state; the support or encouragement within the territory of a state of armed bands bent on incursion into the territory of another state; the fomentation of civil strife or the encouragement of terrorist activities in a state, or the toleration of such by the authorities of another state; acts violating treaties designed to insure peace and security, such as those on arms limitations; the illegal annexation of the territory of another state; intervention by coercive economic or political measures to force the will of another state so as to obtain from it advantages; and finally, acts of genocide.[65]

At the commission meetings a great deal of time was spent by various members in seeking to incorporate within the code offenses which would fall within the concept of indirect aggression and subversion. The Chinese representative desired to include a provision making it a crime to organize, encourage, tolerate, or support a fifth column in another nation.[66] Mr.

Spiropoulos of Greece argued that a fifth column would be criminal only if its direct object was to prepare for an aggression, a viewpoint to which exception was taken.[67] Nevertheless, the inclusion of a special reference to fifth columns was voted down.[68]

Dr. Garcia-Amador of Cuba proposed that coercive intervention be included as an offense,[69] and Dr. Salamanca of Bolivia opined that it should be indicated that intervention also included "the use of the financial resources of the government of another State."[70] The Czechoslovakian representative supported the inclusion, feeling that economic measures could be a use of force in violation of the Charter.[71] On the other hand, others felt that this was too broad, for many acts of an economic nature, even if reprehensible and violating international law, were not necessarily crimes.[72]

A proposal to add subversive activities to the list of offenses was made with the argument that they constituted a special danger to democratic, free governments.[73] In rebuttal Dr. Francois of the Netherlands declared that the term "subversive activities" was far too broad, for this might include ordinary propaganda against an established government; and in true democracies, where there was freedom of expression, private propaganda against a foreign government could not be banned, since in effect it would be a denial of freedom of thought and expression.[74]

In reply to Dr. Francois it was pointed out that the offense of "subversive activities" was comparable to cases of nonmilitary aggression, where a state organized or encouraged subversive activities in another state as acts preparatory to an aggression. Reference was made to a number of inter-American resolutions and declarations which had been adopted to cover such cases, some before World War II to counter Nazi activities in the hemisphere, and others after the war to counter the activities of international communism. The subject had been scientifically studied by the Montevideo Committee on Political Defense and by the Legal Department of the Pan-American Union, and it had been proven by these studies that under the inter-American security system, the organization and encouragement of subversive activities were considered acts of political aggression and were, consequently, international crimes.[75]

Mr. Cordova of Mexico thought that Mr. Francois's arguments were somewhat unjustified, since it was permissible in a democratic state to carry on propaganda against the established government of another nation, but not to attempt to overthrow it by illegal means. These were two distinct concepts which should not be confused. He viewed "subversive activities" as relating only to attempts to overthrow a government by illegal means.[76]

On the other hand, Dr. Lauterpacht of the United Kingdom stated that the international community was no longer a society for the mutual protection of established governments. A revolution might not be a crime against the international community. So long as international society did not effectively guarantee the rights of man against arbitrariness and oppression by governments, it could not oblige states to treat subversive activities, when they did not amount to hostile expeditions, as a crime. He was in agreement with Article 2(4) relating to incursions by armed bands, but felt it would be most regrettable if the commission adopted a provision which might lead to the restriction of freedom of speech and political opinion. States should not allow their territory to be used as a base for armed raids, but propaganda in favor of a political theory was a very different matter.[77]

Mr. Spiropoulos agreed with Dr. Lauterpacht, stating that there was a great difference between the organization of armed bands and subversive activities. Any attempt to ban the latter would run counter to the recent evolution of the guiding principles of the international community which governed the very life of modern states. It was essential that the draft code should not be unacceptable to the states.[78]

The Swedish chairman gave an example from his own experience. About twenty years earlier, the Swedish government had asked him to conduct an inquiry into subversive activities in Sweden and to propose measures to curb them. By the time that inquiry was completed, it had become clear that legislation to curb such activities would inevitably infringe upon fundamental democratic liberties, and that the only result of repressive measures would have been to drive these activities underground. It might be objected that Sweden was a special case, but he did not think so. Any provision against subversive activities merely demonstrated the impotence of a state to deal with the problem such activities created. The organization of armed bands and the fomenting of civil strife, which were the subject matter of paragraphs 4 and 5 of Article 2, were really international crimes; but the term "subversive activities" was so vague that it did not warrant a special paragraph in Article 2.

In rebuttal it was stated that the case mentioned by the chairman referred to internal opposition; the conclusions drawn from the chairman's experience did not therefore necessarily apply to the case of subversive activities directed against a foreign state. Although it was admitted that Dr. Lauterpacht's remarks on the evolution of the international community were certainly pertinent, nevertheless, in the present state of international relations, no peace was possible if states were not protected against subversive activities organized by foreign governments.[79]

It was further declared that as paragraphs 4 and 5 of Article 2 dealt with attempts to overthrow a foreign government by violence, the proposal to add subversive activities to the list of offenses could only be thought of as propaganda, and respect for freedom of speech demanded that any form of propaganda in favor of political opinions should be permitted.[80] The proposal to add subversive activities was defeated by a vote of 7 to 2 with 4 abstentions.[81]

The reasons for abstaining from voting on the overall draft were also of interest. In dealing with this draft, Mr. Edmonds of the United States abstained on the ground that he had been appointed to fill the place of another United States delegate and had arrived so late that he did not have time to consider all aspects of the draft. Nevertheless, he also indicated that he felt the draft's terms were too vague and indefinite to stand the test of statutory political validity. He expressly stated that paragraph 9 of Article 2, a nonintervention clause prohibiting coercive measures of an economic or political character to force another state's will, "appeared to condemn as unjustified interventions practically all the normal manifestations of international life."[82]

Dr. Lauterpacht of the United Kingdom also abstained from voting and dissented expressly from paragraphs 5 and 9 of Article 2, believing that the words "civil strife" were ambiguous. He pointed out that it would be going too far to make criminal the encouragement by authorities of a state of any form of political dissension in other states.[83] Mr. Pal of India also abstained, explaining that while he regarded most of the acts listed as wrongful and reprehensible, still "in the present phase of international development, it would be impossible to punish them in a spirit of justice."[84]

The draft which the International Law Commission adopted was referred to the Sixth Committee for comment. There was widespread agreement in this committee that no final decision on the code could be taken at the time. Therefore the committee adopted a resolution proposing that further consideration of the draft code be postponed until some decision was reached by the General Assembly relating to the question of defining aggression, for it was noted that in its preamble the draft code "raises problems closely related to the definition of aggression." This resolution was adopted by the General Assembly without discussion on December 4, 1954.[85]

Special Committee on the Question of Defining Aggression, 1953

The fact that the 1951 International Law Commission's Draft Code of Offenses Against the Peace and Security of Mankind contained no definition of aggression, together with the fact that the commission's report on its study of a definition of aggression concluded that the concept of aggression could not be defined, caused some head-scratching among members of the General

Assembly. A number of members were dissatisfied with this approach, and the issue of whether or not definition was possible or desirable was sent to the Sixth Committee in 1951.[86]

The Sixth Committee disagreed with the conclusions of the International Law Commission, reporting that it would be very helpful if the United Nations could provide "directives" for international bodies which might be called upon to determine the aggressor. It was, therefore, suggested that the General Assembly instruct the secretary general of the United Nations to report to the next session on the problem of defining aggression, after he received comments from the various nations on both the Draft Code of Offences Against the Peace and Security of Mankind and the International Law Commission's study of the definition of aggression.[87]

The secretary general's report, presented in 1952, indicated that the members of the United Nations were of two minds. Some favored defining aggression, others were opposed. Those in favor were divided into three groups: those who wanted an enumerative definition, those who wanted an abstract definition which would only set forth the constituent elements of aggression, and those who wished to combine both methods into a mixed definition. This report was sent on to the Sixth Committee, which went over the same grounds again, without resolving the issue. But a new element did come out of this discussion—the introduction by various Latin American nations of the idea that any definition of aggression should cover economic, cultural, and ideological aggression. The Sixth Committee could not come to any satisfactory definition of aggression, and it suggested to the General Assembly that a special fifteen-member committee be appointed to produce "draft definitions or draft statements on the notion of aggression" for presentation to the General Assembly. In December, 1952, the General Assembly, noting the need for a more detailed study on the manifold aspects of aggression, appointed such a special committee.[88]

When the special committee began its work, it had before it, in addition to all the other studies previously made by the League of Nations and the United Nations, two working papers presented by the Chinese which gave a general definition of aggression plus a list of typical acts of aggression; a Bolivian working paper which recommended a list of certain acts deemed to be aggression; and a new Soviet text containing definitions of direct, indirect, economic, and ideological aggressions.[89]

Although the majority of the committee members agreed that aggression must be defined in the sense of its usage in the Charter of the United Nations, there was little agreement among them as to what that sense might be. It was generally accepted that the use of armed force against the territorial integrity or political independence of a state in violation of Article 2(4) of the Charter constituted aggression. Accord was also reached on the idea that aggression included the use of force against a territory placed under an international regime as well as against a state. The Chinese delegation expressed the view that in addition to the use of armed force against the political independence or territorial integrity of a state, the use of armed force to establish hegemony over other states should also be considered as aggression.[90] This would appear superfluous. It would seem that an establishment of hegemony would violate political independence or territorial integrity or both.

Some issue was taken with the view that unlawful use of armed force should always be considered aggression. It was pointed out that insignificant uses of armed force such as frontier incidents should not be considered aggression. But the big disagreement arose on the question of whether actions other than the actual use of armed force fall within the Charter's meaning of aggression.[91]

Those who took the view that it was necessary to confine aggression to the illegal use of armed force did so because Article 2(4) called upon the members to refrain from the threat or use of force and did not use words of obligation to prohibit economic, ideological, or other types of intrusions or interferences. Further, it was alleged that the right of self-defense as set forth in Article 51 was permitted only as against armed attack, i.e., armed aggression. It was alleged that since Article 39 spoke of threats to peace, breaches of peace, and aggression, for purposes of Security Council collective measures, economic or ideological methods should really be considered as a threat to peace, not as aggression.[92]

The Iranian delegate disagreed with such restrictive interpretations, declaring that there were forms of aggression other than those involving the use of armed force. He stated: "Any act which served the same ultimate purpose as armed attack or involved the use of coercion to endanger the independence of a State should be considered aggressive."[93]

The Mexican delegate pointed out in this connection that in case of aggression under Article 39 the Security Council was authorized by Article 41 to use measures involving force and measures not involving force as it decided. To him this indicated that aggression could take a form other than armed force, for then resort would be had to measures not involving armed force.[94]

Again, there was disagreement as to whether a threat of the use of armed force could in itself be considered aggression. The point was subject to argument primarily because Article 51 speaks expressly of the right of self-defense against armed attack, making no mention of the threat of armed attack. If self-defense can take place only in face of an aggression, then it can be permitted under this section only against armed aggression or armed attack. Counter views were set forth on the ground that Article 2(4) of the Charter obligates the parties to refrain not only from the use of force, but also from the threat of force. However, even here a *mere* threat to use force would not automatically be sufficient to constitute aggression. The threat must be a threat of an imminent use of armed force, and must also be a threat directed against the territorial integrity or political independence of a state.[95]

The Chinese delegate insisted on calling a threat to use armed force an indirect aggression. His reason for so doing, however, is most unclear. He was of the following opinion:

According to Article 1 of the Charter, a threat to peace was different from a dispute; whereas a dispute was essentially capable of being settled by peaceful means, a threat to the peace implied the possibility of aggression or a threat to use force. A threat to use force should therefore be regarded as indirect aggression.[96]

Apparently he felt that aggression must involve the actual use of armed force, and that threats to the peace which were not actual armed attacks but which might include a threat to use armed force would be indirect aggression because they would not immediately involve a direct use of armed force.

So this again brought to the fore the question of whether indirect aggression should be included in the definition of aggression. Some members opined that indirect aggression could come within the meaning of the Charter only if force or threat of force was involved. Without the element of force indirect aggression could fall only within the concepts of threat to peace or breach of the peace. Others expressed the view that indirect aggression was a form of aggression. The idea of indirect aggression was construed to include subversive interventions. Certain hostile acts or certain forms of complicity in such acts were set forth, such as the organization of armed bands to invade the territory of another state; and other actions to stir up civil strife, including traffic in arms, acts of terrorism, incitation to civil war by propaganda, fifth columnists, and the sending of subversive agents were labeled types of illegal indirect aggression. The Iranian delegate went so far as to say that any intervention in another state's internal or foreign affairs should fall under the heading of indirect aggression, thus apparently including economic aggression and ideological aggression under the classification of indirect aggression.[97]

The developing nations were the main supporters of the notion of economic aggression, which, they said, could have the same consequences as armed aggression, i.e., infringement of the sovereignty of a nation. The Bolivian delegate asserted: "Armed aggression was a recourse to force, economic aggression was a recourse only to pressure, but it could lead a country not only to civil war and loss of independence, but also reduce it to poverty and famine."[98]

The Dominican Republic delegate wanted to include as an indirect form of aggression commercial and economic discriminatory practices by certain countries in world trade.[99] The Iranian delegate took a more restrictive position, confining economic aggression to "[c]oercive economic and political measures taken against a state directly or indirectly and designed to impede the exercise of its sovereignty over its national resources or its efforts toward economic development."[100] The Soviet Union took a similar view, looking upon such aggression as economic pressure.[101]

Those opposed to the notion of economic aggression contended that it would be an extension or amendment of the Charter to include this within the meaning of aggression. They said that economic aggression could not give rise to the exercise of self-defense under Article 51, because this was limited to armed attack; even if all aggression was illegal, not every illegality was aggression. And they asserted that it was unnecessary to classify economic coercion as aggression, for if such coercion constituted a threat to the peace effective action could be taken by the Security Council under that heading of Article 39 without resorting to the aggression label.[102]

The idea of ideological aggression was also subjected to much opposition on grounds similar to those of opposition to other forms not involving the use of armed force. The United States mentioned that "to include any reference to ideological aggression or propaganda in a definition [would afford] a pretext for attacking the freedom of the press."[103]

Even though the committee members agreed that any definition would merely have the status of a recommendation,[104] when the showdown came they failed to agree upon a definition, although that of the Netherlands was included in the committee report.[105] It confined aggression to the threat or use of force for any reason or purpose other than individual or collective self-defense or in pursuance of a decision or recommendation by a competent organ of the United Nations.

Undoubtedly the Soviet draft definition which had been presented to the committee was the most comprehensive. It set forth categories of aggression, indirect aggression, economic aggression, and ideological aggression. Aggression, according to this definition, involved the use of armed force, including support of armed bands which invade the territory of another state. The latter, it must be remembered, has often been deemed to be indirect aggression.

Indirect aggression, according to this Soviet draft, occurs when a state "(a) encourages subversive activity against another State (acts of terrorism, diversion, etc.); (b) promotes the outbreak of civil war within another State; (c) promotes an internal upheaval in another State or a reversal of policy in favor of the aggressor." Economic aggression consists of one of the following acts: "measures of economic pressure taken by a state against another which violate the sovereignty and economic independence of the other and threaten the basis of its economic life; measures taken by a state against another state which prevent it from exploiting or nationalizing its own natural riches; and finally, the subjecting of another state to an economic blockade." Ideological aggression is that whereby a state encourages war propaganda; propaganda in favor of using atomic, biological, chemical, and other weapons of mass destruction; and propaganda which promotes the propagation of fascist-nazi views of racial and national exclusiveness and of hatred and contempt for other people.[106]

China, Mexico, and Bolivia also submitted working papers to the committee. Mexico confined aggression to the direct or indirect use of armed force.[107] She would recognize the so-called indirect, economic, or ideological aggression as aggression only if these involved or were accompanied by the use of armed force.

The Chinese delegation, which had submitted two working papers, recognized aggression as the unlawful use of force, but it also recognized that such force could be armed or unarmed. Its purpose was said to "be the violation, impairment or destruction of the territorial integrity or political independence, or the subversion of political and social order . . ."[108] Moreover, listed as aggression in its first definition were not only waging war and imposing blockades, but also such indirect and subversive activities as planting fifth columnists or subversive agents in a victim state and inciting civil strife by propaganda.

Bolivia listed among other acts of aggression the following acts usually called indirect aggression: support given to armed bands for purposes of invasion, overt or covert inciting of people to rebellion, and action "depriving a state of economic resources derived from the proper conduct of international trade" or endangering its basic economy to a degree whereby its security is affected.[109]

Ninth Session of General Assembly

This report of the Special Committee on the Question of Defining Aggression was referred by the General Assembly in 1954 to the Sixth Committee for further study and report. The Sixth Committee had before it the report of the Special Committee and text of comments on the matter of defining aggression which had been received from various governments.[110] Little that was new emerged from the Sixth Committee's debate. The argument centered primarily upon the question as to whether aggression could be defined, with some delegates reiterating that it was undefinable, others contending that it would be useless or dangerous to define the term, while still others considered a definition not only possible but absolutely necessary. Again the type of definition needed was also argued. The same old arguments pro and con the inclusion of indirect aggression, economic aggression, and ideological aggression within the definition were brought forward.[111] Discord prevailed, and the Sixth Committee recommended to the General Assembly that since the discussions revealed a need to coordinate the views expressed by the member states, another Special Committee should be appointed. This was done, and the new Special Committee was requested to submit a detailed report and draft definition of aggression to the Eleventh Session of the General Assembly.[112]

Special Committee on the Question of Defining Aggression, 1956

Although the new Special Committee had before it reports of previous United Nations discussions as well as previously submitted draft definitions, it replowed the same field. The Soviet Union reintroduced the definition which it had submitted in 1953-54.[113]

Some representatives continued to argue that aggression in Article 39 of the United Nations Charter covered armed aggression only, while others were determined to include indirect aggression as well as economic and ideological aggression. In the Soviet draft, armed aggression was considered the most dangerous type and was the only kind permitting the use of force in self-defense.[114] Peru took exception to this, stating that in its view self-defense was justified against armed attack *and all other* acts of aggression.[115] Yugoslavia argued that provision for aggression of the economic or ideological type could lead to preventive war and that reference to these types in a definition of aggression might precipitate an illegal so-called liberation crusade.[116] China asserted that since the end of World War II subversion had become the most dangerous manifestation of aggression, and that it could not rationally be omitted from any viable definition.

Several other nations presented draft definitions in the form of proposed General Assembly resolutions. Many hours of fruitless discussion ensued.[117] There were criticisms of all the proposals. Certain delegations, the United

States and the United Kingdom, wanted no definition at all. Definition was, however, favored by the majority of committee members, although that majority would limit the definition by excluding forms of aggression not employing force. As a result, economic and ideological aggression were left out of most definitions, as were subversive activities unless linked with a use of force, such as support of armed bands bent upon armed attack.

An anomaly did occur here. Certain of the delegations which characterized aggression as including subversive, economic, and ideological actions not employing force for purposes of Article 39 still rejected any notion that Article 51 permitted the right of at least forceful self-defense against such nonforceful attacks.

Most of the criticism of the definitions were arguments against any definition at all or against the type of definition used, or arguments highlighting exceptions not covered by proposed definitions. But these conclusions can be drawn:

1. Definition was definitely favored by most delegations, with the United States and the United Kingdom opposing any definition and the Netherlands opposing the definition of aggression but proposing a definition of "armed attack."

2. The mixed type of definition gained the support of other delegations with the exception of Iraq.

3. There was some argument, with a view to obtaining the support of the majority of the delegations, to exclude the forms of aggression that do not employ force. Therefore, economic and ideological aggression were excluded. Subversive activities, however, were included when linked with another state and the use of force.[118]

Despite its mandate, this committee, too, was unable to draft a universally acceptable definition.

At its twelfth session in 1957, the General Assembly considered the report of the 1956 Special Committee and by resolution declared that in spite of some success achieved "it was obvious" that other aspects needed to be taken into consideration and that therefore the secretary general should be requested to invite the new states which had been admitted to the United Nations since December, 1955, to express their views on the subject and to renew the request for comments of members who had not previously submitted them. The replies were to be forwarded to a committee composed of representatives of the member states represented on the General Committee.[119]

This committee convened from April 14 to April 24, 1958. The debates were first limited to the nature of the duties of the committee, whether these were of a purely procedural nature or included also the discussion of the essence of the problem of the definition of aggression, and second, the convenience of defining aggression. Inasmuch as the received replies of member states did not indicate any change of attitude, the committee concluded that a resumption of debate in the General Assembly on this problem at this time would bear no results.[120]

The committee met again from April 2 to April 9, 1962. It redebated the scope of its task and the convenience of defining aggression. The majority again favored a definition, but, on the other hand, agreed to postpone the introduction of the subject on the agenda of the General Assembly for another three years. The committee agreed to reconvene again in 1965 unless a request for earlier consideration was received from an absolute majority of its members. The secretary-general was also called upon to request states admitted to the United Nations since the 1959 session to submit their views and to renew his earlier requests for the views of other members.[121]

Deliberations of 1967

As commanded, the Committee on the Question of Defining Aggression met in 1965, but no further action was taken on the problem of definition. It was decided that the committee would convene again in 1967 to consider the matter.[122] During a course of meetings in April, 1967, the committee gave its attention to the subject of the timeliness of a new consideration of the question by the General Assembly. The matter was resolved in December, 1967, by the General Assembly, which adopted a resolution entitled "Need to expedite the drafting of a definition in the light of the present international situation." This resolution established yet another Special Committee on the Question of Defining Aggression to look into the matter and submit a report to the twenty-third session of the Assembly.

Both in the 1967 meetings of the committee and in the General Assembly debate, there was often acrimonious discussion as to whether renewed study of the meaning of aggression should be undertaken. Many of the old arguments for and against were dusted off and reespoused. The communist nations and most of the smaller powers supported renewed efforts at definition, although some of the latter were not sure that the time was propitious and some expressed fears that the effort might be influenced by "tendentious propaganda." As in the past, the western powers were for the most part in opposition on the grounds that definition would be neither practical nor useful, that a definition was not attainable, and that it would not make the United Nations more effective and might detract from maintenance of peace efforts.[123]

Special Committee on the Question of Defining Aggression, 1968-1971

The Special Committee on the Question of Defining Aggression began its deliberations in June, 1968, the deliberations extending into July of that year.[124] After discussing the value of defining or of not defining, the type of definition, and what should be contained in a definition, discussion which also included the bandying about of many charges of aggression against specific states, the committee was finally able to get down to a consideration of two draft declarations on the subject. The first proposal was submitted by twelve states.[125] After extensive paragraphs of preamble, the document proclaimed aggression to be

the use of force in any form by a State or group of States against the people or the territory of another State or group of States or in any way affecting the territorial integrity, sovereignty and political independence of such other State, other than in the exercise of the inherent right of individual or collective self-defense or when undertaken by or under the authority of a competent organ of the United Nations.[126]

Following this general definition, certain acts constituting aggression were enumerated, with an admonition that this listing was not to be considered as precluding the declaration of other acts as aggression. The enumerated acts included declaration of war in violation of the United Nations Charter; invasion; military occupation or annexation of a state by the armed forces of another; armed attack against the territory, territorial waters, or air space of a state by the land, sea, air, or space forces of another; blockade of coasts or ports; bombardment or the use of ballistic missiles or other means of destruction against the people, territory, territorial waters, or airspace of another state; and any use of force so as to prevent a dependent people from exercising its right of self-determination which was declared to be a violation of the Charter of the United Nations. Finally, a broad statement was made that no political, economic, strategic, security, social, ideological, or any other considerations could be invoked as excuse to justify aggressive acts—particularly the internal situation in a state or the acts of its legislative body which would affect international treaties.

The second proposal was submitted by four Latin American states.[127] The first eight articles of this document were concerned primarily with the use of force. Such use was broadly condemned except in the exercise of the right of self-defense or by a competent organ of the United Nations or by a regional agency where authorized by the United Nations Charter. The right to take action in self-defense was limited to instances involving armed attack. Subversive or terroristic acts against a state could be met by "reasonable and adequate steps to safeguard its existence and its institutions." As in the previous draft, the use of force to deprive the right of dependent people to self-determination was said to be a violation of the Charter.

Article 8 proclaimed acts deemed to be direct aggression. They were similar to those stated in the twelve-power draft, such as declaration of war in violation of the Charter; invasion; armed attack against the territory of a state by a state's armed forces; blockade; and bombardment. An additional act of aggression was said to be "[t]he use of atomic, bacteriological or chemical weapons or any other weapon of mass destruction." Again, as in the twelve-power draft, political, economic, strategical, social, or ideological considerations were declared not to justify any acts of aggression.

Specific acts of aggression advanced in both of these proposals are acts characterized as direct aggression; that is, those carried out directly by the state or its armed forces involving the use of armed force. This seems somewhat surprising in that the convergent trend in the 1950s would appear to have been to include not only armed direct aggression, but also armed indirect aggression and aggression not involving the use of arms, such as economic and ideological aggression. That the switch was made here was due to the fact that agreement was prevalent, although not unanimous, that priority should be given at this time to the drafting of a definition of direct aggression, particularly armed aggression.[128] It will be noted that some ambiguity is present in the general definition of the twelve-power draft which would call aggression the use of force in any form, which could be interpreted to include force other than armed force. However, the drafters seemingly intended to limit the definition to armed force. Moreover, some of the members of the committee were actually opposed to an inclusion of elements of indirect aggression, such as the support by a state of armed bands with a purpose of overthrowing the government of another state. The representative of Ghana stated:

Moreover, the Committee's definition should clearly exclude certain actions which would normally be regarded as constituting direct aggression. For instance, the organization and encouragement by a State of armed bands within its territory for the purpose of overthrowing the colonialist or apartheid regime should be justifiable if the Charter of the United Nations and its various pronouncements were to have any meaning.[129]

Indeed, not only was action taken by subject or colonized peoples for their national liberation to be considered legitimate, but the use of force to prevent them from exercising their right to self-determination was to be considered aggression.[130]

The Latin American draft contained a statement on subversive acts. According to the Mexican delegate, the acts were to be defined narrowly as involving a certain use of force, such as a breach of a duty by a state to insure against the organization of armed bands within its territory bent upon invasion of another state.[131] Moreover, the "reasonable steps" which a state could take to insure its existence were unclear. What could be reasonable and adequate steps? Would they be confined to measures against subversion taken within the state's territory, or could steps be taken against the provocateur state?

There was of course much wrangling about both of these drafts. Some delegates believed that indirect aggression, subversion, and terrorism should also be placed within the scope of aggression, as well as economic and ideological aggression. Certain representatives viewed the drafts as deficient because the priority principle—i.e., that the aggressor would be the first state committing any of the acts listed as aggression—was omitted. Criticism was also directed to the fact that the drafts did not apply to political entities which did not fulfill the requisites of statehood. The Canadian and United States representatives stressed the necessity of applicability to a nonstate entity so as to protect against the possibility of its being a victim of aggression as well as to prevent its committing aggression.[132] Some concern was felt because the proposals did not make crystal clear the Security Council's discretionary authority in determining aggression or in maintaining an exclusive authority in that body.[133]

These and other questions were raised as to the two drafts. Thereafter a new combined draft was presented by thirteen nations for consideration.[134] In defining aggression generally, the new draft still confined it to the use of armed force, but such use could be either direct or indirect. The specific acts of armed aggression cited were similar to those presented in the other drafts. In addition, aside from the competence of the United Nations to use force, this draft provided that no considerations other than the exercise of the right of individual or collective self-defense would provide an excuse for use of armed force. Apparently the right of self-defense was even to be precluded to "a state victim in its own territory of subversive and/or terroristic acts by irregular, volunteer or armed bands organized by another state . . . ." Finally, armed aggression was declared to be an international crime, and it was further provided that the Security Council could consider acts other than those named to constitute aggression.

Although this draft did attempt to deal with some of the criticisms and was a compromise, still many of the objections remained and the objectors were not yet satisfied. The Soviet Union noted that lack of remaining time prevented a detailed examination of this third draft. It was, therefore, pro-posed that the General Assembly should authorize the Special Committee to resume its work as soon as possible so that its work on an acceptable draft of a definition could be completed.[135] Thereafter, after consideration by the Sixth Committee, the General Assembly authorized the Special Com-mittee to resume its work on a definition as early as possible in 1969.[136] During February and April, 1969, the second session of the Special Com-mittee again met to struggle with the meaning of aggression, but there were some slight variations on the theme at that time.[137] The United Kingdom and the United States, apparently bowing to majority sentiment in the United Nations, finally changed their stand that it was neither necessary nor desira-ble to arrive at a definition of aggression. Therefore, along with Italy, Japan, Canada, and Australia, they became the sponsors of a six-power draft defi-nition.[138] In spite of this concession, the draft was largely ignored, as the Special Committee spent most of its time considering a Soviet revised draft definition and a revised draft definition submitted by thirteen of the smaller developing nations.[139]

The first operative paragraph of the Russian draft (which again was of the mixed type) stated:

Armed aggression (direct or indirect) is the use by a State, first of armed force against another State contrary to the purposes, principles and provisions of the Charter of the United Nations.[140]

Some objection was raised to this section on the basis that the term aggres-sion in and of itself included both concepts, direct aggression and indirect aggression. It was further stated that the Soviet draft appeared to extend the concept of aggression to acts not involving the use of armed or physical force, because the very term "armed aggression" seemed to imply that there were other forms of aggression within the meaning of the Charter, while actually, it was claimed, the Charter view of aggression was based only on two essential factors: the use of armed force and an attack on the territorial integrity and political independence of another state.[141] In reply to this, other delegates declared that the term "armed aggression" was too limited even in terms of interpreting the United Nations Charter which, it was pro-fessed, recognized other types of aggression, but which limited the right of self-defense solely to cases of armed aggression, that is, armed attack under Article 51. In prohibiting the use of force or the threat of force, it was ar-gued, the United Nations recognized other types of aggression, such as eco-nomic aggression and political pressure, which could be regarded as force-ful aggression even if they took place without armed attack. The concept of force could not be limited to "armed" force only, and hence it was stated that the Charter, by this circuitous reasoning, implied that the concept of aggression involved more than armed attack.[142]

The element of provocation was brought into the discussion when one representative raised the question of whether and how far provocation would exonerate an attacking state from the charge of aggression. It was pointed out that none of the draft definitions which had been submitted took into account the issue of provocation.[143]

Under the thirteen power draft proposal, aggression was defined as the use of armed force by a state against another state affecting the territorial integrity, sovereignty, or political independence of that state. Among its operative paragraphs was one declaring that enforcement action or any use of armed force by regional arrangements or agencies might be resorted to only if there was a decision to that effect by the Security Council. Exception was taken to this statement by a number of representatives who felt that this was an inaccurate interpretation of Article 53 of the Charter, in that it referred to "any use of armed force" whereas Article 53 spoke only of "enforcement action." One of the consequences of this variation was to deny the possibility of collective self-defense through regional agencies as recognized in Article 51 of the Charter.[144]

The thirteen power draft definition was also subjected to critical questioning with reference to an operative paragraph which read:

When a state is a victim in its own territory of subversive and/or terrorists acts by irregular, volunteer, or armed bands organized or supported by another state, it may take all reasonable and adequate steps to safeguard its existence and its institutions, without having recourse to the right of individual or collective self-defense against the other state under Article 51 of the Charter.[145]

It was pointed out that insofar as the reasonable and adequate steps mentioned were strictly internal, there could be no limitation on a state's right of sovereignty to safeguard its existence and institutions from terroristic subversion supported and organized from abroad. But the further attempt to limit the right of self-defense in the face of an aggression of an indirect character would be contrary to both general international law and the international law established by the United Nations Charter. It was argued that to deny the victim of armed subversion the right to determine for itself whether it was justified in exercising its right of self-defense was fraught with many dangers, particularly at a time when armed subversion was increasingly becoming a substitute for the more conventional methods of armed aggression.[146]

Both the Russian draft and the thirteen power draft would define as aggression any resort to chemical and biological weapons as well as resort to weapons of mass destruction.[147] This, of course, was part of a continuing effort to slip into every discussion of force in the United Nations a ban on these weapons. Such a ban would be more appropriate in a treaty dealing directly with these weapons, where the weapons could be carefully defined and regulations for their destruction set forth.[148] It would seem very inappropriate to designate the use of a particular weapon as aggression, for it is not the nature of the weapon involved that constitutes aggression, but rather the circumstances under which weapons are resorted to.[149]

The six power draft backed by the United States and the United Kingdom did not contain a preamble, and was strictly limited to interpreting the word *aggression* as it was thought to be used in the Charter of the United Nations.[150] It was a mixed type of definition consisting mainly of a general description of aggression ("the use of force in international relations, overt or covert, direct or indirect, by a state against the territorial integrity or political independence of any other state")[151] together with an exemplary but not conclusive list of descriptive acts of aggression such as invasion; bombardment; inflicting physical destruction through the use of other forms of armed force; organizing, supporting, or directing armed bands or irregular volunteer forces that make incursion or infiltrate into another state; organizing, supporting, or directing violent civil strife or acts of terrorism in another state; or organizing, supporting, or directing subversive activities aimed at the violent overthrow of the government of another state.[152] This latter phrase was objected to by some on the grounds that it was difficult, in this age of ideological clashes, to distinguish between internal revolts or dissident internal movements and externally supported antiestablishment violent dissent. And even where such distinction between internal and external support could be made, it was claimed that it was often impossible to trace such external support directly to a state rather than to a loosely organized and governmentally unconnected revolutionary spirit sweeping the globe today.[153]

Another criticism leveled at the six power draft was its failure to enumerate among acts of aggression the use of chemical and biological weapons or the use of weapons of mass destruction.[154]

On March 28, 1969, noting the common will of the members of the Special Committee to continue consideration of the question of defining aggression, it was recommended to the General Assembly that the Special Committee should be encouraged to resume its task in 1970.[155] The General Assembly adopted a resolution to that effect, with the addendum that in view of the fact that 1970 was the twenty-fifth anniversary of the United Nations, it might be suitable to aim at a final solution in that year of the difficult and tedious problem of defining aggression as used in the United Nations Charter.[156]

During its 1970 session, the Special Committee established a Working Group of eight members representing the sponsors of the three draft proposals which had been submitted during the 1969 session: Britain, Cyprus, Ecuador, Egypt, France, Ghana, the Soviet Union, and the United States.[157] Because the Working Group was unable to complete its report to the Special Committee prior to the end of the 1970 session, the General Assembly decided that the Special Committee should resume its work as early as possible in 1971.[158]

In accordance with this resolution, the Special Committee reestablished the Working Group composed of the same member states as in the 1970 session.[159] The Working Group submitted two successive reports to the Special Committee. The first report reflected the outcome of the Working Group's discussions on the general definition of aggression and the principle of priority.[160] The second report reflected the results of the Working Group's discussions on the questions of political entities other than states, the legitimate use of force, aggressive intent, acts proposed for inclusion, proportionality, legal consequences of aggression and the right of peoples to self-determination.[161]

The Working Group sought to combine the various positions adopted by its members in a single text by offering different versions of the text through the use of square brackets. The phrases which were not acceptable to all members appeared in brackets.

As to the general definition of aggression, the following text was worked out:

Aggression is the use of armed force [however exerted] by a State against [another State] [or in any way affecting] [the sovereignty or] the territorial integrity [including territorial waters and airspace] or political independence of another state, or in any manner inconsistent with the purposes of the United Nations.[162]

Apparently the greatest problem of the Working Group centered around the phrase [however exerted] which was felt to be absolutely unacceptable by some members, and absolutely vital and essential by others.[163]

All members of the Working Group were in favor of incorporating the principle of priority into the definition of aggression, but some members regarded it as a determinative factor while others felt that it should be merely taken into account. Again, in discussing the principle of priority, the Working Group resorted to the use of brackets for phrases which were not acceptable to all members:

[Without prejudice to the powers and duties of the Security Council] [in determining whether] an act referred to in . . . constitutes aggression [due weight shall be given to the question whether] [it shall be established] if it was committed by a state which so acted first [against another State in violation of the Charter].[164]

Views on the first report submitted by the Working Group to the Special Committee ranged from gratitude of the committee for clarification of the approaches of different delegations to opinions that the deliberations of the Working Group indicated that no change had occurred from positions previously taken by the various delegations. Some praised the device of placing controversial phrases in brackets; others felt that the fundamental differences remained, and that the use of brackets as a drafting device led to even greater ambiguities.[165]

Because of lack of time the Special Committee was unable to examine the Working Group's second report. Consequently the General Assembly agreed to extend the life of the Special Committee for another year.[166] Again, apparently, a great deal of ground had been covered and nothing had been accomplished.

The legal adviser of the United States delegation pointed out in a rather confusing manner that with the expulsion of the Republic of China and the admission of Communist China to the United Nations, a new element relating to the definition of aggression might appear on the United Nations scene. "Some day when they [the Communist Chinese] wake up and discover that there is an exercise on 'aggression' they might say something. I should think 'aggression' would be right up their alley."[167]

CHAPTER III

THE CONCEPT

THE PROBLEM

AN EXAMINATION of the concept of aggression as it has fared before international jurists and assemblages makes it manifest that the meanings attributed to this phenomenon range all over the lot. Without reviewing in detail all the opinions, one can group the most important positions as those which would limit aggression to a direct use of armed force, extended by some to an indirect use as well. Others do not agree to these limits, advancing the position that aggression signifies not only armed aggression, but also other actions both indirect and direct such as economic aggression, ideological aggression, and subversion. Some insist that if an internationally acceptable definition of aggression excludes the economic and ideological forms, it should at least include subversive actions, which have often been regarded as the most blatant form of indirect aggression. Others, however, view subversion in a dual light, accepting subversive activities for the overthrow of "colonialists or apartheid regimes" as perfectly legal. Indeed, armed action on the part of a state to put down liberation efforts by its subject peoples would be considered by some as aggression. The only area of agreement, then, is that aggression does cover a direct illegal armed attack by a state against the territorial integrity or political sovereignty of another state, an attack which is something more than *de minimis* in character.

Aggression as used in Article 39 of the Charter of the United Nations is an undefined act, but when it takes place it will allow collective coercive measures by the international community to maintain or restore international peace and security.[1] Although members of the United Nations are forbidden to resort to force or the threat of force against the territorial integrity or political independence of any state, there are exceptions to this prohibition, namely the use of force in the exercise of individual or collective self-defense or in participation in collective measures taken to enforce and maintain the peace as laid down by the Security Council or by the General Assembly.[2] Hence, not only war but other measures involving the use of force which fall short of war would appear to become, under the Charter, illegal.

This prohibition of the illegal use of force has, since the coming into existence of the United Nations, become the predicate for any definition of aggression. And it is from this concept of aggression as an illegal use of force that the idea of indirect aggression was developed.[3] It was almost an afterthought, arising out of sheer pragmatism, for it was discovered that the purpose of war or of the use of armed force might be achieved by other means short of the use of armed force, and these means came to be designated as indirect aggression or subversion. Many objectives for which armed force was used in the past are now being realized through nonmilitary, nonforceful pressures. Used in a most intensive manner by the totalitarian states, the so-called indirect aggressions have come to be considered more dangerous than the direct or military type of aggression. On the theory that the defense of independence might be weakened by limiting the right to use armed force against armed attack only, and that by fifth columns, infiltration, foreign-organized conspiracies, hostile propaganda, and other like activities states might succeed in drawing other states into their orbit, it has been suggested that within the meaning of the term *aggression* should be included *indirect aggression.*[4]

Private law since the Romans has admitted that violence could be both physical and moral (*vis absoluta* and *vis compulsiva*).[5] The latter would signify a coercion able to destroy a man's freedom of will and determination by a threat of an immediate and grave evil. Threat of use of force was admitted as a case of moral violence. This Roman private law theory came to be recognized in international law. The cases of the Austrian Anschluss (by Germany) and the communist take-over of Czechoslovakia have proved that the freedom of a state is prone to disappear when there is an imminent threat of the use of force made against it by certain other powerful nations.[6] Such a threat of the use of force, being only a threat, has been considered an indirect use of force. Many started calling it indirect aggression.

Other means of coercion were also admitted to be effective in imposing a foreign will. Economic measures were found to be frequently used means to force a state to accept the directives of another state. The term "economic aggression" was therefore coined.[7] It was discovered that modern means of propaganda, when cleverly used, were able to produce alarming results in other states, particularly when such propaganda incited to war, or appealed to a foreign people to overthrow their government or to change their regimes, institutions, or policies. This, then, came to be called ideological aggression.[8]

The term indirect aggression was also applied to the cases in which a state, without admitting any responsibility in the hostilities deriving from it, used armed force against another state through a third state or through groups of its own nationals pretending to be "volunteers," or through other armed groups of foreigners or nationals.[9] So, too, the aiding, encouragement, or toleration of such groups within a state's territory and the supplying of them with arms was considered indirect aggression. Indirect then became equivalent to nonofficial participation in hostilities and subversion.[10]

What was first called aggression, the use of force, came to be direct aggression, and what was first called indirect aggression, an indirect use of armed force through third-party groups, came to include within it the concepts of economic, ideological, or cultural aggression. A further expansion took place when some used the expression of aggression as synonymous with intervention in the affairs of another state. It has even been used to mean any violation of international law by a state, and has been carried so far as to mean a violation of the vital interests of a state.[11] It may be that the notion of aggression has come to mean nothing simply because it means too much.

Since the voices are discordant and authorities differ as to the meaning of aggression, exploration into the various elements of aggression and forms and acts which have been designated at one time or another as aggression becomes requisite. Determination can thus be made as to which of those hostile activities directed by members of the society of nations against their fellows can be considered or should be considered under present international conditions as within the meaning of aggression at international law.

APPLICABLE ENTITIES

The word *state* is generally used in marking out a meaning of aggression at international law, either as the aggressor or the victim of aggression. Since the state has been the prime recipient of rights and duties at international law, it is the sovereign state which is usually regarded as the aggressor or the one against whom the aggression is committed.[12] But there are certain other entities which are subjects of international rights and duties—for example, international organizations. Thus, international agencies like the United Nations or the Organization of American States can be considered as aggressors if they engage in delictual activities of a coercive nature against a state so as to endanger its security.[13] These organizations in turn can also be victims of aggression if an aggressor embarks upon aggressive acts against their forces which are acting legitimately to maintain the peace.[14]

Other entities, such as territories under an international regime and unrecognized states, have been marked out for inclusion. Moreover, there has arisen a tendency in the United Nations to place responsibility for unlawful aggression upon *de facto* governments.[15]

Difficulty does prevail, however, in attempts to extend the meaning of an aggressor and his victim beyond the usual international law definition of *state*, for the inclusion of other entities simply complicates matters. Some claim that a definition should conform to the United Nations Charter, confining the meaning to states only. But this rationale is imperfect, for the Charter does not define *aggressor* or *aggression*, nor does it expressly limit the commission of aggression to states. It is true that the members of the United Nations to whom the Charter's terms are primarily directed are spoken of in the Charter as states. Still entities which are not sovereign or independent states, such as the Byelorussian and Ukrainian Soviet Socialist Republics, have become and remain members of the world organization. Could these entities be designated as aggressors or subjects of aggression apart from the Soviet Union?

The Iraqi draft definition submitted in 1956 sought to solve the problem by a proposal that aggression could emanate not only from a state or group of states, but also from a government or group of governments against a state or group of states, "or against the conditions of existence of the peoples of a Government or group of Governments."[17] But this does not really clarify much, for vagueness and overbreadth occur if the term "government" is used. "Government" has a multitude of meanings and classifications, e.g., a local or state governmental unit within the sovereign state. Should such a local governmental entity be characterized an aggressor if it acts against the central or national organ and vice versa? If the meaning of *government* is limited to the government of an international entity, as was probably intended by the framers of the draft, confusion still exists. Would the meaning be confined to a *de jure* government, a *de facto* government? Would it include also certain dependent governments, United Nations trusteeship governments, or even governments-in-exile?

A 1969 proposal attempting to make aggression applicable to entities bound by international law as to the use of force and not generally recognized as states, or whose status at international law might be questionable in another way, provided that

Any act which would constitute aggression by or against a State likewise constitutes aggression when committed by a State or other political entity delimited by international boundaries or internationally agreed lines of demarcation against any state or other political entity so delimited and not subject to its authority.[18]

This proposal would eliminate the objection sometimes voiced that extension of the meaning of aggressor or the victim of aggression to political entities other than states would permit an interpretation to include an opposition party in a democratic state, inasmuch as the language quoted above makes it clear that the political entity cannot be subject to the authority of the state. The proposal would encompass within its terms a *de facto* state with delimited boundaries as well as entities whose boundaries had been delimited by international agreement, like North and South Vietnam. Moreover, trusteeship territories would fall within this language, and so perhaps would belligerents engaged in a civil war. Belligerency is carried on between two political bodies exercising authority over persons within a determined territory. Some dispute might arise in some cases concerning both *de facto* states and belligerents as to the territorial requirement, inasmuch as boundaries may not have become firmly jelled and may not have been demarcated by agreement at the time of the act of aggression.

Insurgents would appear not to be encompassed within the terms of this draft. Insurgency may have become war in a material sense; still, it may exist when the insurgents are not yet in control of determined or demarcated territory.[19] However, insurgents could commit acts against other states which would be in the nature of aggression and which could be called aggression. Insurgency is often said to be unlike belligerency, in that it is not a status under international law.[20] Therefore it gives rise to no rights or obligations. This may be too broad, for certain wrongs committed by insurgents against foreign states have been deemed unlawful. Moreover, it has been pointed out that measures of protection by a foreign state against acts of insurgents are legitimate acts of self-defense which if in conformity with international law are not open to criticism.[21] Since acts of aggression are usually thought to give rise to a right of self-defense it would logically then follow that if such acts are conducted by insurgents they could be called aggression.

Aggression is often described as being perpetrated against the territory or political independence of a state as well as against its people and land, sea, or air forces.[22] What is most often brought to mind when attention is directed to aggression is an attack against the territory of a state, a violation of territorial integrity. Territory of the state would of course include its territorial waters and air space, and these areas are often mentioned in draft proposals. Unfortunately, the extent of territorial water or air space is not spelled out in these proposals, and since such extent is subject to much dispute, confusion can result as to the characterization of certain acts taking place on the sea or in the air as aggression.[23] For example, would Peru's actions against United States fishing vessels within a two-hundred-mile distance from Peru's shores, but outside the traditional three- to twelve-mile limit, be an armed aggression or an act of internal police, in view of the fact that Peru claims her territorial waters extend to a distance of two hundred miles?[24]

Political independence has two aspects, the freedom of action possessed by each state to conduct its relations with other states as it deems fit—external independence—and the right of self-government by the state or the supreme authority to control all persons and things within its boundaries—internal independence.[25] Political independence would thus have broader significance than aggression against territorial integrity, for the external independence of a state can be violated without at the same time impairing its territorial integrity.

Some question has been raised as to aggression against the people of a state over and above aggression against territorial integrity. To include "people" is a departure from the language of the United Nations Charter, which prohibits the use of force against territorial integrity or political independence only.[26] On the other hand, it has been stated: "Aggression is bound to be conceived as perpetrated against the territory and against the people under the jurisdiction of the state victim, and aimed at the submission or destruction of any forces opposing resistance to the aggression."[27] Any attack against the people of a state within the boundaries of that state would be a violation of territorial integrity. In this sense the use of "people" would be superfluous. Only when the people of a state are on the high seas, in space, or within the territory of another state would an addition be made to a definition of aggression by inclusion of the people of a state as subjects of aggression. If a people in these areas were subjected to acts otherwise considered as aggression, there would be no reason why their state of citizenship could not be considered as having been a victim of aggression.[28] Citizens of a state outside the territory of a state are still subject to its jurisdiction. Moreover, a state's right of self-defense extends to protection of its nationals from attack in the territory of a foreign state where the foreign state is unable or unwilling to extend the necessary protection. A state can meet attack not only against its territory, its armed forces, vessels, or aircraft, but also against its citizens.[29]

DELICTS AND INTENT

Aggression is a delictual conduct carried on by one state against another. Thus all conduct which affects the interest of a state in a significant and adverse way is not aggression.[30] To be aggression the conduct must be illegal, an illegality under international law. Nevertheless, not all illegal conduct is to be considered as aggression. It must be action—armed or unarmed —which violates the essential legal rights of a state, which endangers that state's security, and which permits that state to resort to the right of self-defense.[31]

As has been seen, in its initial stages aggression was a neutral military technical word implying only first armed attack.[32] As time went by it acquired an additional gloss—an implied modifying adjective, *unprovoked* attack.[33] But even now the nature and extent of provocation have not been completely resolved in the defining of the word. In 1968, for example, the Australian representative, posed the issue of exoneration from a charge of aggression. It should be noted that he called provocation a matter for "political appraisal":

The concept of aggression, in the ordinary meaning of the term, was relatively simple and implied "unprovoked attack." But the word "unprovoked" alone was a source of endless controversy. The Charter prohibited, in international relations the use of force except, *inter alia,* in the exercise of the inherent right of self-defense. But how long, for instance could Governments ignore frontier incidents or neighboring troop movements? How much did that depend on the relative size and strength of the States concerned? By what yardstick could the patience of a Government or the emotional stability of a people be measured? These were not matters for legal definition, but for political appraisal. Ultimately to determine the existence of an act of aggression and to identify the aggressor was to determine whether the act in question was one of attack or of defense. In the view of his delegation, that could be achieved by the exercise of discretion in assessing a total situation, but not by the mere process of definition.[34]

One of the most important international mutual defense arrangements in which provocation plays a role in the determination of the aggressor is the Inter-American Treaty of Reciprocal Assistance (the Rio Treaty). Article 9 of that instrument declares that an unprovoked attack by a state against the territory, the people, or the land, sea, or air forces of another state may be characterized as an aggression.[35] The use of the term "unprovoked" is misleading, for by reading Article 9 in conjunction with Article 3 which sets forth the right of self-defense against armed attack one might conclude that no right of self-defense exists if one state provokes another state to attack it; for in that case the provoked attacking state would not be an aggressor. This may or may not be true, depending upon the nature of the provocation. The United Nations Charter and the Rio Treaty prohibit the use of force except in accord with Article 51 of the Charter, which recognizes the inherent right of individual or collective self-defense against an armed attack.[36] This is taken to mean an illegal attack. International law adds the additional qualification that self-defense is to be exercised against delictual conduct attributable to a state. Unfriendly acts or attitudes of a state toward another state which do not impinge upon international law can well be provocative, but they cannot justify a reaction in self-defense by the aggrieved state, or bar an exercise of the right of self-defense by the provoking state against an attack by the aggrieved state.[37] Moreover, the provoked state would, even though provoked, still be an aggressor. On the other hand, if the provocateur commits an act against a state which violates the essential rights upon which the security of that state depends, then the provoked state can react in an exercise of the right of self-defense. The provoked state would be acting legitimately and would not be considered an aggressor. That label would fall upon the state provocateur.

Those provisions in various draft definitions of aggression to the effect that political, economic, strategical, social, or ideological considerations cannot justify acts of aggression would seem to be superfluous.[38] Nothing can justify aggression. Political and economic acts and the like if not delictual could not be used as legal justification for aggression even though they might provoke it. On the other hand, language of certain drafts which goes further might well be of significance. When such language declares that "no other considerations may be invoked as justification, particularly the internal situation in a state or any legislative act affecting international treaties," a change in meaning and in law occurs.[39] Broad prohibitions of "any other considerations" as justification would also include and prohibit illegal acts or considerations which might otherwise be thought of as aggression. Moreover, internal situations may well violate international law, and acts which breach treaties do violate international law. Both of these in some instances could be considered as aggression and could justify certain retaliatory actions, unless aggression is to be confined to illegal armed force.

Often said to be an element of aggression in addition to illegal acts is unlawful intent.[40] Although intent to commit aggression is usually required before aggression occurs, still it must be emphasized that the word *intent* is a legal word not to be confused with *motive*. Intent is the purpose to use particular means to effect a result and shows the existence of will or deliberation in the act, while motive is the moving power which impels to action for a definite result. Motive is not usually an essential element of a wrong, for a good motive does not prevent an act from being illegal, nor does a bad motive make a legal action illegal. To be intentional, an invasion of another's interest need not be inspired by malice or ill will on the actor's part toward the other. Thus the reason or apparent lack of reason why a state commits aggression against another state is unimportant.[41]

Furthermore, a state cannot always defend its action on the ground that it did not have the necessary *animus* or intent required to make its action aggression. In law it is properly inferred that one who does an act willfully intends the natural and proximate consequences of the act. A state is thus presumed to have willed the results of its action. When a state is under a legal duty and it breaches that duty with knowledge that the consequences will endanger the essential rights upon which the security of another state depends, the state which breached its duty intends the consequences just as truly as if it intended to commit aggression, i.e., to do the actual thing which resulted.[42]

In discussion of certain of the draft definitions of aggression it has been asserted that unlawful intent as a component of aggression can be inferred from statements defining aggression as the use of force against the territorial integrity or political independence of a state and from listings of forms of force constituting aggression. In answer to this it is noted that intention is too important to be inferred in relation to the meaning of aggression and should be expressly designated as such.[43] Other drafts, without mentioning the word *intention*, declare that aggression consists of use of force for certain designs or purposes or intentions such as to diminish a state's territory or change its boundaries, to alter its government, or to interfere with its conduct of its affairs. These listings have been criticized on the grounds that it would be impossible to list all possible unlawful purposes or intentions.[44]

Another viewpoint takes issue with the inclusion of intention in the definition at all, either explicitly or implicitly, and would seek an exclusion of this subjective element. If intention is a part of aggression, then aggressive intention could not be found against one whose act was occasioned by a reasonable and good-faith mistake, or even when hostilities break out by accident—when, for example, in a period of tension, frontier incidents occur by the action of troops of opposing nations along the border despite the fact that neither government may have willed the hostilities or desired their occurrence. Since intention as a component permits the introduction of such defenses, calling for a determination of the subjective element of intent, there is fear of the advancement of bad-faith pleas of excuse which would permit an aggressor to claim that its action was legitimate or lacked the requisite intention—a situation described as "highly dangerous in the present state of the international community."[45] It has been said: "If that element [intent] were included in the definition it might tempt an aggressor to rely on such spurious defences as anticipatory self-defence, duress *per minas* or mistake. No legitimate defence of mistake could be open to a State inadvertently unleashing a nuclear attack."[46]

The advancement of spurious claims and defenses is always a possibility in disputed situations. It is the task of the legal process to separate truth from falsity. The fact that the international legal process may not be sufficiently advanced to make a differentiation between *bona fides* and *mala fides* would seem a thing apart from the content and meaning of the legal rule. In actuality there would appear to be nothing to prevent the Security Council or other international agency from making the determination. If the reason for the exclusion is difficulty of proving, the following statement is of interest: "If the facts of the case were really so unclear that the Security Council could not determine even that the act was intentional, i.e., calculated to inflict the harm which it in fact inflicted, then presumably no one would wish the Security Council to decide that aggression had occurred."[47]

Opponents also contend that the definition of aggression should conform to the United Nations Charter and that Article 2(4) of that instrument in forbidding the use of force does not speak of intent. Therefore it would not limit the use of force to an intentional use. This argument hardly holds water. The force prohibited by Article 2(4) is force inconsistent with the purposes of the Charter. It is hardly possible to understand a use of force in honest mistakes as inconsistent with such purposes.[48]

ARMED AND UNARMED

The traditional doctrine of aggression refers to the use of armed force in international relations contrary to an international obligation. Interpretations of aggression as it appears to various members reading the United Nations Charter vary greatly, but it must be remembered that although a number of draft resolutions were introduced to extend the term *aggression* to actions not involving the direct use of force, no such resolution has received a sufficient majority to be adopted.[49]

On the other hand, the draft definitions do stress as aggression that aggression which is carried out directly by a state or its armed forces and which involves the employment of armed force against the territory, people, armed forces, ships, or aircraft of another state. Specifically armed attacks, invasions, blockades, forcible annexations of territory, and military occupation have all been acknowledged as acts of aggression. For example, upon the invasion of Finland by troops of the Soviet Union the Assembly of the League in December, 1939, adopted a resolution condemning the Soviet Union for the commission of aggression against Finland by failing to observe special political agreements with Finland, the Pact of Paris, and Article 12 of the League Covenant.[50] The Nuremburg and Tokyo Tribunals, although having no definition of aggression formulated for them in advance, were confronted with the task of finding liability for commission of crimes against the peace which included the "planning, preparation, initiation or

waging of a war of aggression."[51] It is clear that the tribunals viewed aggressive war as demanding actual armed attack or invasion. A take-over of
a country without the use of armed force by a mere threat of such use accompanied by fifth-column and subversive activities was not called aggressive
war, but premeditated aggressive steps in furthering the plan to wage aggressive war against other countries.[52] Another instance of designation of
armed attack as aggression by an international body was that committed
by the forces of North Korea upon South Korea in which Communist China
later joined.[53] This brought forth a resolution by the General Assembly of
the United Nations in 1951, wherein that body found

... that the Central People's Government of the Peoples' Republic of China, by
giving direct aid and assistance to those who are already committing aggression
in Korea and by engaging in hostilities against United Nations forces there, has
itself engaged in aggression in Korea.[54]

These examples of international action are all in accord with the traditional doctrine of aggression which refers to the use of armed force in
international relations contrary to an international obligation. Following this
classical approach, certain jurists and statesmen will admit of no aggression
unless armed force is involved. To some an illegal threat of the use of
armed force if imminent would also be included, although others would exclude illegal imminent threat from the term "armed attack" under Article
51 of the United Nations Charter, for it is feared that to permit individual
or collective self-defense against a threat of armed attack would endanger
peace by authorizing preventive war.[55]

One finds this restrictive attitude, which confines aggression to the use
of force and which rather grudgingly extends it to the threat of such use,
well expressed by Quincy Wright:

An act of aggression is the use or threat to use armed forces across an internationally recognized frontier, for which a government, *de facto* or *de jure,* is
responsible because of an act or negligence, unless justified by a necessity for
individual or collective self-defense, by the authority of the United Nations to
restore international peace and security, or by consent of the state within whose
territory armed force is being used.[56]

From this definition Professor Wright can draw only one logical conclusion,
i.e. that Articles 2(4), 39, and 51 of the Charter of the United Nations, in
prohibiting the threat of or use of force, in making aggression a *casus foe-
deris* for collective action, and in limiting self-defense to armed attack,
signify that aggression means armed force or threat thereof, and, conse-

quently, hostile acts such as propaganda, infiltration, or subversion cannot be included within the meaning.[57] A principal reason given for such a restrictive view is that military action by states or the United Nations designed to stop nonforceful action could not be justified by virtue of Article 39 and Article 51 of the Charter.

Professor Sohn agrees with Professor Wright that the term aggression should be confined to the use of armed force.[58] He believes, however, that indirect aggression as well as economic and ideological aggression should be classified as acts relating to threats to the peace or breaches of the peace without the moral stigma of being called outright aggression. Under Sohn's view, economic, ideological, and other acts of indirect aggression may also give rise to Security Council action under Article 39, which speaks of threats to the peace and breaches of the peace as well as aggression, or may also give rise to action by the General Assembly under the Uniting for Peace Resolution, which speaks of breach of the peace.[59] Such United Nations' action could be taken at least to an extent not involving military action. This analysis, of course, is somewhat contrary to Wright's approach, which altogether denies the applicability of Article 39 to cases of indirect aggression.

A primary reason for opposition to the inclusion of acts of indirect aggression, such as subversion and economic or ideological aggression, in a definition of aggression has been and is that such inclusion would suggest a right to resort to war or armed force in self-defense against acts not involving the use of armed force. It was felt that in such event peace would be endangered rather than promoted.[60]

Dr. Pompe tells us, in speaking of the United Nations Charter and the meaning of aggression, that "not only war but all use of force by the States is forbidden, and it is obvious that this interdiction must be the basis of and the point of departure for every attempt to define aggression."[61] Again, he says: "It is, thus, the necessity of defense on which the right of defense is dependent which determines the existence of aggression."[62] Later he declares:

The States cannot be allowed to answer with military measures every kind of foreign support or influence on internal attacks against the established political order and the legitimate government. Foreign propaganda against a government, economic or financial boycott, political support of revolutionary parties and still less that of certain groups within a government could hardly justify a military reaction, be it on the part of the victim or on the part of the international community.[63]

Aggression as a legal concept has significance in two most important instances: (1) when the Security Council of the United Nations, acting under Article 39 of the Charter, or the General Assembly, acting under the Uniting for Peace Resolution, is called upon to react in the face of aggression with collective measures to maintain or restore peace; and (2) when a state may have recourse legally to the right of self-defense under Article 51 of the United Nations Charter.[64] Restriction of the meaning of aggression to actual armed attack or use of force under the present collective security system is motivated by the belief that the states' right to use armed force in an exercise of the individual and collective right of self-defense should be and has been limited, in accordance with the literal meaning of Article 51 of the United Nations Charter, to an actual armed aggression only. The command of the Charter to its members to refrain from the use or threat of force against the territorial integrity or political independence of any state has been interpreted literally as a prohibition of the use or threat of physical force or armed force.[65] With regard to coercion or attempted coercion of states by means not involving the use of armed force, such as economic or psychological methods, Goodrich and Hambro have pointed out that these methods "may be undesirable and contrary to certain of the declared purposes of the United Nations, but the obligations of this paragraph [Article 2(4)] is not directed against action of this kind."[66] This categorized thinking takes the narrow interpretation of threat or use of force, combines it with the idea that self-defense is the necessary corollary of aggression, and arrives at the conclusion that the sole condition on which the right of self-defense can be exercised is limited to armed attack. Even a threat of armed attack is not sufficient. A leading author in the field of international law states it as follows: "The Charter confines the right of self-defense to the case of an armed attack as distinguished from anticipated attack or from various forms of unfriendly conduct falling short of armed attack."[67]

Moreover, jurists taking the restrictive view have thought it erroneous to define aggression broadly and outside a context of force, for if this were done the Security Council under Article 39 or the General Assembly under Uniting for Peace would be permitted to order and recommend a military action in a situation where armed force would not be appropriate. A collective measure involving the use of force would be too drastic a measure to be used against compulsive illegal action by a state not involving a use of force. If these jurists are correct, then those acts which are often classified as indirect aggression would not be so classified except for that indirect aggression actually involving the use of armed force where a state acts through others who commit the armed attack. And yet it is the so-called indirect aggression which has been said to be far more dangerous than direct aggression to the sovereign existence of the state today, as well as to world peace. The limitations of aggression only to instances of armed attack and possible threats thereof is too narrow. There have been refinements in the techniques of aggression in the twentieth century, and the trend appears to be to wipe out the territorial integrity and political independence of a state by means far more subtle than direct use of armed force.[68] The use and/or threat of armed force cannot be said to exhaust acts which may be characterized as aggression, and the concept would seem to have been extended to acts of states which are often called indirect aggression, such as the fomenting of civil strife in other nations through the use of hostile propaganda, fifth columns, infiltration of the political parties of the state sought to be destroyed or controlled, or the organization, encouragement, and toleration of armed bands to operate against another state, as well as intervention by means of economic and political coercion to obtain advantages. Protection against these methods either through collective security or, failing that, self-help is as imperative as safeguards against direct armed aggression.[69]

Actually, there is no need to confine aggression to an illegal use of armed force. As has been pointed out, a definition of aggression becomes important in two principal contexts. The first has to do with the action to be taken by the collective security system in case of aggression. The United Nations Charter enjoins the Security Council to decide upon measures which are to be taken to maintain or restore international peace and security when it determines the existence of any threat to the peace, breach of the peace, or act of aggression.[70] Moreover, the General Assembly is called upon when the Security Council, because of lack of unanimity of the permanent members, fails to act, in case of threat to or breach of the peace or act of aggression, to recommend to the members collective measures, "including in the case of a breach of the peace or act of aggression the use of armed force when necessary, to maintain or restore international peace and security."[71] In these instances these United Nations organs are called upon to make a determination as to the meaning of aggression. Are they legally limited by a definition of aggression to a meaning involving the use of armed force only? If aggression is always to be identified with self-defense, and if the right of self-defense is limited to a use of armed force against armed force, then aggression must involve only an illegal use of force.

It is argued, however, that in defining aggression one must look to the purpose or the function of the definition, and that a definition changes depending upon the purpose for which it is to be used or the function which it is to serve. It is contended that the concepts of self-defense and aggression for purposes of determining when the machinery of collective security will operate in the interests of the maintenance of international peace should not be identifiable or correlated with the concept of self-defense, for self-defense is a legal concept and one concerned with allocating legal responsibility. The General Assembly and the Security Council, as executive agencies, when called upon under the Uniting for Peace Resolution and Article 39 to act for the restoration of international peace and security through collective action, are not concerned with setting out legal responsibility or with designating the culprit guilty of the delict. These bodies are intervening to maintain and restore international peace and security, and their enforcement action need not be taken against illegal conduct only.[72] The Charter appears to contain no rule that measures are to be taken against the country which is legally wrong. The Security Council, for example, is free to decide according to the necessities of the situation against whom the enforcement action shall be directed. It should take into consideration all surrounding factors, primarily the practical means of ending the situation speedily in the interests of the maintenance or restoration of peace and security.[73]

Even though it can be argued that there need be no correlation between self-defense and aggression for purposes of the collective action function, still it seems somewhat foolish to create differing definitions for differing purposes. Two or more definitions of aggression, depending upon the purpose to which the definition is to be put, add confusion to an already confused subject. It is doubtful if the drafters of the Charter had in mind varying meanings to be attached to the word *aggression*. Moreover, neither the Security Council nor the General Assembly has seen fit to set forth differing definitions. In reality there appears to be little necessity for differing meanings for purposes of Article 39, whether a more elastic or more restrictive definition is sought. Even if aggression for purposes of Article 51, which authorizes the right of individual and collective self-defense, is to be confined to a use of armed force, and even if it is believed that the Security Council and the General Assembly are or should be empowered to take measures in the face of lesser offenses, there is still no need to define those lesser offenses as aggression to permit such measures, for the Security Council can act just as easily by the language of Article 39 when there is a threat to the peace or a breach of the peace (which such lesser offenses could and probably would involve) as when an aggression occurs. The General Assembly can act when an aggression or a breach of the peace occurs. Collective measures are not limited to aggression only.[74]

The argument does not hold water that the collective security agencies of the United Nations are limited to a definition of aggression involving use of armed force or threat thereof, because Article 39 is concerned with situations in which United Nations military action can be taken and military action would be too drastic except as against illegal use of force by a state. True, the Security Council may decide that the appropriate measure in the case of a threat to the peace, or breach of the peace, or act of aggression is the use of armed force. But it may also decide that the appropriate measures to maintain and restore international peace and security are measures not involving the use of armed force—measures such as interruption of communications, economic relations, or diplomatic relations which are authorized by the United Nations Charter. There may be no reason for the United Nations to meet an aggression not involving the use of armed force with armed force. A lesser measure may be appropriate, and this is authorized by the Charter. To argue that aggression is confined to use of force simply because the United Nations *may react* with the use of force is specious. The Security Council's authority to determine the presence of coercive acts and to impose enforcement measures is not restricted to acts of military coercion, nor are its enforcement acts conditioned upon a finding of a use or threat of armed force. The same can be said as to the General Assembly's authority under Uniting for Peace.[75]

Moreover, it would seem that aggression is complementary to or interrelated with self-defense, although some no longer consider this to be true. Traditionally, it has been so considered. The necessity of a legal defense has been the determining factor of an aggression. The present-day notion that aggression can be committed without the victim's acquiring the right of self-defense seems to arise from those who wish to extend the concept of aggression from strict aggression—that is, aggression involving the use of illegal armed force—to other acts endangering the security of a state. It is reasoned, mistakenly we believe, that the exercise of the right of self-defense, which it is concluded always involves a use of force, is requisite only against a use of force. This idea is particularly prevalent in view of the United Nations Charter, which would seem to limit the right of self-defense (apparently the right to use armed force) under Article 51 to armed attack only.[76]

Under international law states are under a mutual duty to respect one another's sovereignty and are bound not to violate one another's rights. As an exception, however, certain intrusions into the sphere of interests of another state committed by a state for the purpose of self-defense are not prohibited by the law of nations.[77] Article 51 of the United Nations Charter is an outcropping of the concept of an inherent right of self-defense—a special and necessary form of self-help. There have, however, been conflicting opinions at general international law, as well as under the United

Nations Charter, as to when the right arises. Some authorities would limit the exercise of this right to a situation of protection against an actual illegitimate attack or when such an attack is imminently impending. Following this line of authority, self-defense is self-help against a specific violation of the law against the illegal use of force, not against other violations. It is recognized by national law as applicable to individuals and by international law as applicable to nations. It is impossible for any collective security system, national or international, to prevent all illegal attacks upon its subjects; and in case of such an attack, if the attacked subject were always required to wait for the enforcement authorities to take action he would be doomed.[78] This restricted viewpoint outlines the prerequisites of legitimate self-defense as follows: the armed attack, actual or impending, must be objectively illegal; the state exercising the right of self-defense must show a direct and immediate danger; the act of self-defense must not be excessive, going no farther than to avert or suppress the attack; and it must not be continued after the needs of defense have been met. To equate aggression with this narrow view of self-defense would be to limit the concept in effect to actual illegal armed attack or an illegal threat of armed attack which is imminent.[79]

It is possible, however, to view self-defense at international law as wider in its scope, and some authorities do not restrict the right as against illegal use of force only, but extend it to other delinquencies where it is exercised in a preventive and nonretributive manner.[80] It is claimed that a state may legitimately resort to the right of self-defense for its protection when its essential rights are endangered by delictual conduct of another state. The danger to these rights must be unlawful, it must be serious, and it must be actual or so imminent that the necessity to resort to self-defense is instant and overwhelming. In addition, the exercise of the right is conditioned upon the absence of other lawful means of protection and the measures used must be reasonable, limited to averting the illegal danger to the safety of the wronged state and proportionate to that danger.[81] Such a view of self-defense, in stressing the fact of reasonable and proportionate measures to avert the danger, recognizes that measures used in the exercise of the right of self-defense by the wronged state may be of a lesser nature than that of armed force. Armed force might not and probably would not be proportionate when used to avert an illegal act which does not involve the use of armed force but which still endangers in a serious and imminent way the rights and security of the state. Although the classic example of self-defense is a meeting of force with force, still there would appear to be no reason why the defending state cannot react with lesser measures not involving force if the state is acting to protect its rights and is not taking punitive or retributive action in the form of sanctions or reprisals.[82]

This broader approach leans heavily upon the conception that international law is at present an immature law lacking a centralized law enforcement machinery, and consequently such a legal system must permit a large measure of unilateral action for the protection against illegal violation of those legal rights which are necessary for the security of the state.[83] If the international enforcement machinery cannot safeguard such rights either at all or in an expeditious and prompt manner, the subject of the legal system must be empowered to protect them by its own action. When international society matures to a point where centralized machinery for securing the rights of its subjects is available and efficacious, then the right of self-defense should be circumscribed to a point where it can be considered as legitimate only to avert and to protect against an illegal use of force which is permitted as of necessity by the most developed legal systems.[84] Considering a state's right to protect itself by measures of self-defense against violation of those legal rights necessary for the security of the state, and considering further that aggression is correlated with self-defense, we see then that aggression becomes more than an illegal use of force and includes any illicit conduct by a state which seriously endangers essential rights of another state upon which that state's security depends.

Opinions exist, however, that no matter what might have been the rule at general international law, the right of self-defense as recognized by the United Nations Charter is limited to action after armed attack has occurred. It is concluded that the United Nations Charter does alter the right of self-defense as it existed at general international law, restricting it to instances where there has actually been an armed attack by an aggressor, and neither an imminent attack nor other violation of a state's legally protected interests is thought sufficient to invoke the right under Article 51 of the Charter, or sufficient to constitute aggression.[85]

Issue has been taken with this severely limited view of the right of self-defense on the grounds that Charter interpretation does not necessarily warrant such a circumscribed conclusion. To the contrary, it is contended that the Charter does not change the right of self-defense as it existed at international law; hence, until the Security Council takes measures to maintain international peace and security, a member state is free to take action, including the use of force, for its own security and protection on its own volition not only against an armed attack, but also against a threat of an armed attack when imminent, as well as against violations of a state's other essential legal interests.[86]

It is reasoned that Article 51 is only a declaratory article designed to preserve the right of self-defense, not to limit it, and containing no additional obligations.[87] It is then maintained that Article 2(4), the relevant article of obligation here, is not inconsistent with the traditional right of self-defense, for interim measures taken by a state to protect and defend its vital legal rights cannot be considered—even when involving a threat or use of force—as being taken against the territorial integrity or political independence of the state committing the delict or inconsistent with the purposes of the United Nations.[88] From a more practical point of view, it is pointed out that the political necessities of modern international life force a recognition by general international law, as well as the international law of the United Nations Charter, of a right of self-defense of broader scope; for to limit such a right to armed attack in the absence of a truly effective collective security system could well be to circumscribe the legal right of a state to protect against its own destruction. A state can hardly be expected to wait for this actual attack in the face of imminent threat, for if it did so the state might be so paralyzed by the attack that it could no longer render resistance. Nor can it be expected to sit idly by in the face of other types of aggression and illegal acts which jeopardize its security with no legal right to resort to self-defense.[89] As Professor McDougal has pointed out, a rejection of

a right of self-defense in any and all contexts not exhibiting overt violence and even against the most intense uses of non-military instruments—may, under the same conditions of the present world, amount to requiring a target state to be the sedentary fowl in an international turkey-shoot.[90]

Following this line of thought and linking aggression with self-defense, we may say that aggression is the violation of those essential legal rights upon which the security of the state depends, creating the necessity of protection by resort to the right of self-defense. To be legal, the protective measures employed must be proportionate to the danger. Aggression can, therefore, be regarded as delictual conduct which violates and endangers the right of territorial integrity or political independence or sovereignty, thus placing the security of the state in danger. As such it would include the classical or traditional type of aggression, i.e., direct military operations of an illegal nature by one state against another, as well as other illegal acts which do not involve the use of armed force directed against a state and endangering its essential security.

But does not the inclusion of acts not involving the use of armed force within the definition of aggression endanger rather than promote world peace, in that such inclusion justifies war or use of force in self-defense against what have been considered rather insignificant acts of indirect aggression, such as economic or ideological aggression or other subversive acts? As has been emphasized many times, such acts may not be so insignificant, for they can be as detrimental to a state as those involving use of force. In addition, the point does not seem to be well taken. Not only must self-defense be adequate to be effective, but it must also be proportionate to justify an act which would otherwise be basically illegal. The use of force as a reaction to an aggression not involving force would seldom be proportionate, but, as Dr. Bowett states, "there is no rule of law to say that it can never be so. . . ." In extremely rare cases, in which the defending state would be subjected to an extremely stringent burden of proof, self-defense might justify the use of force against an aggression not involving force.[92] Bowett discusses the possibility of such a situation in the area of economic aggression where a state is "pursuing a course which leads to the economic strangulation of another state."[93]

The problem of what is necessary and proportionate in an exercise of the right of self-defense to repel acts of subversion or indirect nonviolent aggression may be an uncertain one, and the answer may be difficult to ascertain.[94] Obviously if such acts of subversive aggression are carried out with such a degree of efficiency and intensity as to create in the state against which they are directed a reasonable expectation of an overthrow of the established social order and its legitimate government, counteraction by military means—that is, striking at the foreign base of subversion—may be the only means of defense. It may be noted in this connection that the Organization of American States adopted a declaration on July 26, 1964, which would permit the members alone or in a group to use armed force against subversive activities and actions directed by a state to undermine the governments of other states of the Western Hemisphere.[95]

While many jurists do limit the reference of aggression to coercion by military instruments, Professor McDougal makes "no such postulation as to the types of instruments by which coercion may be accelerated to such an intensity."[96] It can happen that economic, ideological, and diplomatic strategies, particularly when used against a background of military threat and strength, may force the state subjected to such coercion to resort to a military strike. Thus to McDougal the important aspect of the problem lies in the cumulative intensity of the coercion applied rather than in its modalities. The determination is to be made from the point of view of the state subjected to the coercion; that is, the reasonable expectation or apprehension of the target state.[97]

If the test for the use of force against coercion of a nonmilitary nature is necessity and proportionality, the opponents of this doctrine may raise the objection that these tests may be abused. McDougal rejects all such criticisms with the argument that these tests are "in no greater degree susceptible of abuse here than in any other contexts" and that "susceptibility to abuse is a common property of all legal standards and rules."[98]

DIRECT AND INDIRECT

Aggression of the classic type was thought to have occurred when armed force was used against a state by regular military units of another.[99] Such illegal use of armed force taken to reduce a state and its peoples to submission has traditionally been designated direct aggression or simply aggression. More ingenious types of illicit coercion have also been exerted by states against their fellows, types which have been indirect in nature and which have been characterized as indirect aggression.[100] As discussed by jurists and statesmen, indirect aggression would seem to have two prime meanings: (1) delictual acts armed or unarmed and conducted vicariously by the aggressor state through third parties which endanger the essential rights of a state, rights upon which its security depends, and (2) delictual acts taken directly by the governing authorities of a state against another state or vicariously through third-party groups which do not involve the use of armed force, but which do endanger the essential rights of a state upon which its security depends. No direct military operations by the regular armed forces of a state are involved in either case; therefore the aggression can be regarded as an indirect method of constraint carried on by the aggressor state.

Hostile and illicit conduct committed vicariously by a state through the medium of others is a well-known type of indirect aggression.[101] The third-party agents who engage in the aggressive conduct against a state may be groups who are aided, abetted, and organized in the aggressor state's own territory or outside its boundaries—for example, in the territory of the victim, or in the territory of a third state, or even outside the territory of a state on the high seas, or possibly even in outer space. The third party may be composed of private persons who are nationals or non-nationals of the aggressor, or the third party may be another state.[102] Vicarious participation in actual hostilities or preparation therefor smacks of indirect aggression. A state aiding and abetting the commission of aggression will by such conduct become an aggressor.[103] Thus indirect aggression has been called "aggression by proxy,"[104] and as connoted here it takes place when a party acts illegally against a state at the behest of another state with the latter's support and instigation to alter or maintain the condition of things in the former state. The instigating state, the state responsible for the aggressive action, is committing a delict. That state thereby becomes an aggressor, the principal aggressor.

Indirect aggression as vicarious aggression follows a dictionary distinction between the terms *direct* and *indirect*. *Direct* is defined as an unbroken connection, as something bearing straight upon the object, or as the absence of any intervening medium or influences.[105] Thus where the aggressive conduct is the state's own it would bear straight upon the victim state; the connection would be unbroken. Consequently such conduct is a direct aggression. If the aggressive acts take place through third parties they take place through an intervening medium. They do not bear directly in an unbroken line upon the victim. They are indirect; hence they constitute indirect aggression.

The phrase *indirect aggression* in its early connotation was applied to vicarious aggression or aggression committed through the medium of a third party,[106] but its meaning was limited solely to an indirect use of armed force only. This viewpoint continues. Recently, for example, indirect aggression was so defined in the following words:

The use by a State of armed force by sending armed bands, mercenaries, terrorists or saboteurs to the territory of another State and engagement in other forms of subversive activity involving the use of armed force with the aim of promoting an internal upheaval in another State or a reversal of policy in favor of the aggressor shall be considered an act of indirect aggression.[107]

From this definition, the state, in order to commit indirect aggression, does not use its own armed forces to encroach upon a foreign territory or peoples, but operates through third parties, armed persons, who act against the other state, apparently but not in reality on their own initiative.

As has been seen earlier in this study, the Disarmament Conference of 1932-33,[108] without using the terms direct or indirect, described an aggressor as a state first declaring war upon another state or subjecting another state to invasion or attack with its land, naval, or air forces, as well as a state which has supported the formation within its territory of armed bands which have invaded another state's territory, or which has refused upon request of the invaded state to take in its own territory all means to deprive the bands of assistance and protection.[109] An aggressor supporting and assisting armed bands which have invaded another state's territory came to be known as an indirect aggressor, for in Kelsen's words indirect aggression consists of

the supporting by a state of the revolutionary forces fighting against the legitimate government of another state, the arming by a state of organized bands for offensive purposes against another state, the sending by a state of so-called "volunteers" to engage in hostilities against another state, the non-prevention by a neutral state of its own nationals from participating as volunteers in a civil or international war against another state . . . the undertaking or encouragement by a state of terrorist activities in another state or the toleration by a state of organized activities calculated to result in terrorist acts in another state.[110]

Both of these definitions would still find the phenomenon to exist in a context of force only, albeit by third party groups who are aided, abetted, supported, or protected by another state, this state being designated as an aggressor. Certain authorities, however, would not view indirect or vicarious aggression so narrowly, but would extend its meaning to include not only acts committed with armed force by third-party groups, but also hostile and illegal conduct of such third parties not involving the use of armed force if these illegal acts endanger the essential security of the state.[111] Aid and support given by a state to foment civil strife in another state would be considered as indirect aggression even before an armed rebellion occurs in that state or even if it does not occur. Ideological aggression or economic aggression directed by a state against another through intermediaries could also be designated indirect aggression.

In the definition of aggression presented by the Soviet Union in 1954, support given by a state to armed bands for the invasion of the territory of another state or failure upon request of the invaded state to cease and desist from such support within its territory was labeled aggression.[112] Thus, vicarious aggression committed with a use of armed force would be considered by the Soviets as aggression, not indirect aggression. According to this Soviet definition, the encouragement of subversive activity against a state, such as acts of terrorism or diversion, the promotion of the outbreak of civil war in another state, and the promotion of internal upheaval or a change of policy in another state so as to favor the aggressor would fall in the category of indirect aggression. Subversive acts, fomentation of civil strife, and change of policy might well result in a use of armed force, but with the exception of terrorism such acts would not in themselves involve a use of armed force. However, if the subversion results in invasion by armed bands, then according to the Soviets we have aggression, not indirect aggression. Since internal upheaval may be instigated directly by the governing authorities of a state or indirectly through a third-party medium, it follows that the Russians do not base their determination as to direct or indirect aggression on the fact of the vicarious commission of certain hostile and illegal acts against a state. To them indirect aggression consists of subversive acts, fomentation of civil strife, and reversal of policy in a state in favor of the aggressor. Moreover, the Soviets make no direct or indirect distinction as to ideological or economic aggression, for the Soviet draft lists these activities quite separately and calls them simply ideological aggression and economic aggression.

In more recent times the term *indirect aggression* has been used in another sense, as that aggression which does not involve the use of armed force.[113] Consequently, unarmed aggressive acts, whether performed through intermediaries or not, are placed in the indirect category. Acts of the armed variety, whether performed through third-party groups or not, are designated as direct aggression, or simply as aggression. It would seem that the characterization of aggression through means other than by a use of force as indirect aggression is founded upon a notion that direct aggression is defined as taking place through a use of armed force only. Acts of an aggressive character in which no force is used, such as those of an economic or ideological nature, automatically become indirect aggression.

It would seem that the maintenance of a distinction between direct and indirect aggression is rather unimportant. Either a conduct is aggression or it is not. If the view is followed that aggression is the use of armed force only, then armed force through third parties is also aggression with the same consequences, and the qualifying adjective *indirect* can be dropped. On the other hand, if aggression is thought of as including not only armed force, but also other illegal acts endangering a state's security, then again the term *indirect* can be dropped in reference to the latter, and all can fall within the definition of aggression.

CHAPTER FOUR

THE EXTENSION OF THE CONCEPT

ALTHOUGH CLASSICAL AGGRESSION has generally been thought to involve direct military operations by regular national forces under government control, today subjugation and control of peoples may well result from resort to nonmilitary methods. Economic pressures on the other states; demands couched in traditional diplomatic terms but laden with implied threats to compel action or inaction; fifth column activities; the endless propaganda harangue urging another state's peoples to rise against their government; the aiding and abetting of rebel bands intent on overthrowing another government; and a wide range of other modern techniques must be included in the concept of aggression in so far as they are delicts at international law, for they are directed against the sovereign independence of a state.

Thus other forms and acts of an illegal coercive nature are subsumed under the rubric of aggression, and when one state resorts to interventionary and subversive conduct against another state or utilizes ideological and economic coercive patterns against another state, such conduct, in many instances, falls within the modern expanded meaning of aggression.

INTERVENTIONARY ACTS

Intervention in the internal or external affairs of a state has been said to constitute aggression.[1] Customary international law has long prohibited illegal intervention in a state's affairs.[2] The Charter of the Organization of American States, for example, spelled out the prohibition by proscribing intervention in the internal or external affairs of a state, directly or indirectly, for any reason whatever.[3] The principle is applicable not only to armed force but also to any other form of interference or attempted threat against the personality of a state or its political, economic, and cultural elements. The use by states of coercive measures of an economic or political character to force the sovereign will of another state and obtain from it advantages of any kind is also forbidden.[4]

In even more certain and detailed terms, a 1965 resolution of the General Assembly condemned all forms of intervention. This resolution declares in part:

1. No State has the right to intervene, directly or indirectly, for any reason whatever, in the internal or external affairs of any other State. Consequently armed intervention as well as all other forms of interference or attempted threats against the personality of the State or against its political, economic and cultural elements, are condemned;

2. No State may use or encourage the use of economic, political or any other type of measures to coerce another State in order to obtain from it the subordination of the exercise of its sovereign rights or to secure from it advantages of any kind. Also, no State shall organize, assist, foment, finance, incite or tolerate subversive, terrorist or armed activities directed to the violent overthrow of the regime of another State, or interfere in civil strife in another state. . . .[5]

These words do not mention aggression. Subversive acts directed to the overthrow of a foreign government are banned, as well as direct and indirect intervention; and these acts have often been called aggression, usually of an indirect nature. The preliminary clauses of the resolution would recognize armed intervention as synonymous with aggression. Armed intervention may involve a direct or indirect use of force, and an indirect use of force has for the most part been considered as an indirect aggression. For purposes of the resolution, would the latter fall within the aegis of indirect intervention, which the resolution prohibits and which the preliminary clauses declare, along with direct intervention and subversion, to be contrary to the principles and purposes of the United Nations Charter? Does the terminology mean to confine aggression, direct or indirect, to the use of armed force, direct or indirect, or can it include other interventionary acts not involving the use of armed force? Can direct or indirect intervention be equated with direct or indirect aggression? Is subversion indirect aggression or indirect intervention—or is it *sui generis*? The prohibition of subversion and intervention is attributed by the General Assembly to the necessity of protecting the independence of the sovereign state, its existence, its internal and external self-determination, and thereby to further the maintenance of peace.[6] The interdiction of aggression at international law rests upon the same grounds.[7] Query: can intervention and aggression be considered as one and the same?

There must be some overlapping of the concept of intervention and the concept of aggression. This was recognized by the Council of the Organization of American States when it found that indirect involvement by states in revolutionary situations in other states and their fomenting of civil strife in those states violated the nonintervention principles of the Americas. The Council stated that if such facts should persist or recur they would necessitate the application of hemispheric measures of collective security "[t]o ensure the inviolability or the integrity of the territory or the sovereignty or the political independence of any American state against *aggression* on the part of any state or group of states." (Italics supplied.)[8] The Secretary General of the OAS, in speaking of this Council action, stated:

It is almost the same as saying that intervention as condemned in [inter-American treaties] and conventions, is one of the acts of aggression that give occasion for applying the measures contemplated by the Treaty of Reciprocal Assistance. No future meeting of the Organ of Consultation in similar cases, could fail to be guided by this criterion if there should be any doubt as to the application of the Rio de Janeiro Treaty, or if it should be necessary to define the aggressor in the circumstances covered by Articles 6, 7, and 9, of that Treaty. Indeed, the Council was acting under the power of Article 9, which authorizes it to characterize acts other than armed attack and invasion as acts of aggression.[9]

Thus there is a relationship between intervention and aggression. But are the terms synonymous? As has been seen, aggression consists of a substantial amount of illegal coercion against a target state by which the aggressor state seeks effectively to alter or maintain the condition of things within the other nation. The coercive conduct must be designed and intended to bring about in the target state a policy change that is favorable to the aggressor or to prevent an unfavorable policy change in the target state; i.e., the aggressive conduct must involve the use of coercive measures to force the sovereign will of another state and obtain advantages therefrom. Such activities are also included in the meaning of intervention. Thus it is probably safe to say that any aggression, whether described as direct or indirect, is an intervention. Nevertheless, not all interventions can be considered aggression.[10]

Whether one state's illegal conduct against another involves the direct use of armed force, whether it is committed indirectly and vicariously through third party groups, or whether it is illegal governmental action not involving the use of armed force, it is still aggressive conduct by which the aggressor seeks to impose its will upon another state so as to lead to an interference with its domestic affairs or destruction of its national independence or its territorial integrity. As such, the aggression is an illegal intervention.[11] But intervention may be distinguished from aggression. Intervention is defined as any interference by a state in the affairs of another state which is meant or intended to compel certain action or inaction by which the intervening state imposes or seeks to impose its will.[12] This may seem similar to the concept of aggression, but aggression requires an additional element. For conduct to fall under the opprobrium of aggression, there must be an illegal intervention directed against the political independence or territorial integrity or sovereignty of a state, of such seriousness as to endanger the security of the state and thereby permit it to protect itself with defensive measures.[13] Aggression is always illegal,[14] while intervention may be legal or illegal depending upon the surrounding circumstances. For example, proportionate interventionary reprisals for violation of international legal duties are not considered illegal by most publicists.[15] Consequently, to equate aggression and intervention in all instances is patently inaccurate.

SUBVERSIVE ACTS

During the debates in the various commissions and committees of the United Nations there has been a great deal of discussion as to whether or not subversion or subversive activities qualify as aggression. Some states more or less tacitly agree that certain subversive activities fall within the concept of aggression, even though discord prevails as to what specific activities are to be included.[16] On the other hand, there is a hard core of resistance to the inclusion of subversion or subversive activities as being terms in themselves too vague and nebulous and too indefinable to be of any assistance whatsoever in arriving at a universally acceptable definition of aggression.[17]

Prior to World War II, subversive activities were thought to cover cases where states attempted to achieve certain political ends of fomenting civil strife in another state or by supporting rebellion against the legally established government of another state by giving to the rebels supplies of personnel, training facilities, war materials, or munitions and by engaging in hostile propaganda against the victim state and its government.[18] A host of hostile activities were considered illegal, including such things as financial support given by a state or by persons subject to its authority for purposes of instigating and supporting civil strife and rebellion in another state; the use of a state's governmental resources and personnel to train and equip with weapons and munitions of war rebel groups, guerrillas, and terrorists so that their activities might be directed to the overthrow of a government of another state through violent strife in that state; the giving of safe-haven or sanctuary to such subversive groups within its national territory; permitting hostile military expeditions, armed bands, and terroristic groups to form within its territory for attack upon another state in order to topple the latter's government; and finally, suffering or encouraging volunteers to leave its territory to engage in civil strife abroad.[19]

By the beginning of World War II, the concept of subversion had been expanded to include the attempt of one state to weaken or overthrow the government of another by means of infiltration of its governmental apparatus with conspirators who strongly opposed the domestic policy of their own government and willingly served as clandestine instruments in the conduct of an alien state's foreign policy. Crucial to the success of such subversive activities, it was recognized, was the psychological problem of destroying bonds of loyalty that bound a citizen to his government and replacing this loyalty by a willingness to follow the commands of the alien state.[20] Thus this extension of subversion, it was felt, would always be a limited type of illegality because only a fringe element would be enticed into the enemy camp.

But with increased militancy of modern ideologies, new lines of division, cutting horizontally through state units instead of leaving them separated vertically from each other at their frontiers, have now become the vogue. Under such political-ideological alignments, subversive activities are no longer seen in many quarters as advancing the foreign policy of a nation or nations, but rather are thought to advance universal human values, i.e., the specific ideological theory adhered to.[21] As the Russian poet V. Pecherin has put it:

> How sweet it is to hate one's native land
> Eagerly awaiting its destruction
> And in the destruction of the fatherland
> To see the dawn of world awakening.[22]

Under such seductive political-ideological alignments, doubts can be placed in the hearts of great masses of citizens who are ever seeking new solutions for present-day social challenges: aliens may turn out to be friends, while citizens may be more treacherous than enemy aliens. The fact that the present age is one of great social change and revolution would indicate that no society is free from internal divisions and deep animosities, in which philosophical and ideological tenets may invoke deeper loyalties than traditional notions of nationalism and national sovereignty.[23] In instances where political-ideological loyalties take priority over national state loyalties, the potential for converting disaffections into subversive elements is very great.

Therefore, subversion as a modern method of international conflict goes far beyond the mere infiltration of governmental organizations. It encompasses open as well as devious underground attempts to penetrate, influence, and control critical nongovernmental groups and organizations; it spreads a web of conspiratorial activities throughout a nation, using a great variety of techniques to increase legitimate internal agitation and to transform loyal into disloyal or at least into disgruntled elements. It uses both concealed and open propaganda and psychological means to induce the target audience to adopt a certain viewpoint or to behave in a manner which will benefit the propaganda source. It resorts to open political activity in insisting that its ideological orientation is not a trick of propaganda, but the absolute truth and the only way to human salvation.[24] It resorts to underground political activity through active and fanatical believers in the enemy's camp.[25]

Today subversion ranges from externally instigated sabotage and espionage, through advocacy of disobedience to law, to small incidents of disaffection which may concern only a very narrow sector of the community and thus can have no more than a nuisance value, but which when repeated and multiplied eventually give rise to discontent and contempt for prevailing conditions which can be directed against the target government and its leaders. Subversion generally involves sustained and coordinated efforts by a foreign government or an alien political group to seize, preserve, or extend power against a defined ideological enemy, through all acts short of a shooting war by regular military forces, but not excluding the threat of such a war.[26] Over and above innumerable propaganda techniques, it embraces diverse forms of coercion and violence, such as strikes, riots, economic constraint, subsidies for guerrilla or proxy warfare, and, when necessary, kidnapping or assassination of enemy elites. Its purpose is to discredit, displace, and neutralize an opponent, to destroy a competing ideology and to reduce its adherents to political impotence.[27] Subversion consequently extends from one nebulous gray zone into the other gray zone of international relations, i.e., from areas where it becomes almost impossible to distinguish subversive activities from those of direct aggression on the one hand, to the other end of the spectrum where subversion is called modern diplomacy.

There has been some attempt to distinguish diplomacy from subversion by stating that diplomacy seeks the achievement of international political objectives by exerting influence upon the decision-makers of the target state, while subversion seeks to change the decision-makers themselves. Wyckoff declares:

Subversion can succeed where diplomacy has failed. Subversion exceeds the bounds of diplomacy in that it employs methods which diplomacy abhors; it does not wince at assassination, riot, pillage, and arson, if it believes these to be useful in the attainment of its ends. Subversion is a form of war. It may include the use of propaganda . . . to sway the thinking and action of influential social groups, especially attempting to discredit the leadership of the target area, labeling it as the "tool" of . . . any convenient target for emotional hatred. By inflaming passion, the purveyors of violent propaganda can stir up peaceful citizens so that in minutes they are transformed into a terrifying mob. The art of subversion has developed the technique of the manipulation of mobs to a high degree.[28]

Distinctions between diplomacy and subversion might have been valid in more ordinary times, but at present a new methodology has entered into the field of traditional diplomacy and has transformed it from a harmonizing and accommodating instrument used to adjust differences between states into a technique of attack skillfully employed to keep disputes alive rather than to resolve them. This new diplomacy, conducted in extremely vituperative language, is so closely intermeshed with economic, psychological, and military pressures, including the indiscriminate threats of armed attack— even nuclear armed attack—that it is difficult, if not impossible, to determine where diplomacy ends and aggression or subversion begins.[29]

In an attempt to avoid the terms subversion or subversive activities, certain authorities now use the phrase *internal aggression* instead.[30] And internal aggression is then defined as an attack by one state against the internal order of another state, usually through an attempt to overthrow or to harass the government by promoting civil strife and internal upheaval in the victim state.[31] In general such internal aggression would include the aiding or influencing by a state of hostile and illegal conduct against the established political order and government of another state. It is a form of subversion limited to conduct directed against a state's internal order.[32] Subversion is generally considered to be a broader term and designates all illegal activities, whether direct or indirect, overt or covert, conducted under the auspices of the authorities of a state and calculated to overthrow the existing government or public order of another state. Although subversion is at times used synonymously with internal aggression, it is thought that the confining of subversion to acts endangering the internal order of a state may be too narrow an interpretation.[33] An intervention directed at a change or overthrow of the external order could also be considered subversionary and aggressive. For example, a state's incitement of the peoples of other states to compel their governments to withdraw from a mutual security system or to breach a treaty of mutual defense or to break away from a bilateral or multilateral treaty creating a collective system of an economic nature could be considered a subversive intervention against the external order of the state involved.[34]

On the international level the Organization of American States has recognized subversion as endangering not only the internal security of the American states, but also the international order of the Americas, i.e., the inter-American system and the political defense of the Americas.[35] External independence—the power of a state to determine the relations it desires to maintain with other states without interference—is as fundamental as is internal independence. No valid distinction can be made between subversive acts directed against a state's internal order and those directed against its external order.

Of interest is the attempt in recent times to exempt subversionary activity for a certain purpose from the meaning of aggression while the same activity conducted for another purpose would remain within the definition.[36] This is exemplified by Article III of the Charter of the Organization of African Unity, which declared on the one hand the adherence of member states to the principle of non-intervention in the internal affairs of other states, according to the principle of respect for the sovereignty and territorial integrity of each state, and also unreservedly condemned—no matter what the nature of the act—"subversive activities on the part of neighboring states or any other state."[37] But the charter goes on to say that at the same time all the contracting states adhere to the principles of respect for the inalienable right of each state to independent existence, and that they pledge absolute dedication to the total emancipation of the African territories which are still dependent.[38]

While there may be no incompatibility between non-intervention in internal affairs and absolute dedication to total emancipation of colonial African territories, as long as only legal means are used to secure such total emancipation, there is incompatibility between non-intervention and the use of illegal means amounting to subversive aggression to secure such emancipation. And in the light of other conference action, such as the establishment of a committee of nine nations, the Liberation Coordination Committee,[39] with the avowed purpose of gathering and disbursing financial assistance to groups seeking to overthrow the metropolitan power, there seems to be a direct conflict between the established law and the actions of the African nations, which, in their dedication to African emancipation, would resort to all means to effectuate it including aggression—direct or indirect.

In 1957 the French delegate declared before the United Nations that the League of Arab States was supplying Algerian guerrillas with monetary aid and weapons in their fight for independence from France.[40] Such acts, whether committed by a single nation or by a group of nations banded together in international organization, were declared by the French to violate established principles of the Charter of the United Nations, which imposed on member states the obligation to live together in peace as good neighbors.[41] The French delegate quoted Article 2(4) of the United Nations Charter, which prohibits members from threatening or using force against the territorial integrity of another state, and also pointed out that the General Assembly's Essentials for Peace Resolution called upon every nation to refrain from any threats or acts, direct or indirect, aimed at impairing the freedom, independence, or territorial integrity of any state, and from fomenting civil strife in any state.[42] He also noted that the African-Asian States, at their Bandung Conference held in 1955, had endorsed a resolution which declared that all nations were under a duty to respect the sovereignty and territorial integrity of other nations, and were not to interfere or intervene in the domestic affairs of another nation.[43]

The Saudi Arabian delegate, in his reply to the French accusations,[44] flatly declared that it was the duty of the Arab world to sponsor the cause of Algeria against France, by all means feasible, because Algeria was part of the Arab homeland. As further justification he highlighted the undeniable fact that all liberation movements attempting to shake off colonial rule had received assistance and support from abroad in one form or another. He pointed out that "most of the States represented in the [First] Committee had either given or received such assistance."[45] This latter argument, if valid, would permit governmental financial assistance to any rebellious group of another state to be considered legal, for all civil strife can be called "liberation" from something or other.

Draft proposals of definitions of aggression and statements of representatives of certain nations during the 1968-69 deliberations of the Special Committee on the Question of Defining Aggression would appear to reach a conclusion similar to that reached by the African organization and the Saudi Arabian delegate.[46] Most of the drafts contained provisions that the use of force to deprive dependent peoples of their inherent right to self-determination violated the United Nations Charter. The Soviet draft would recognize a right of dependent people to use force to exercise their right of self-determination.[47] After setting forth acts considered to be aggression, it concluded with a statement that "[n]othing in the foregoing shall prevent the use of armed force in accordance with the Charter of the United Nations, including its use by dependent peoples in order to exercise their inherent right of self determination."[48]

It may be that these words are merely a recognition of the fact that civil strife under international law is a domestic question, in no way of and by itself an international wrong or delict. Thus there is a right of a people of a state to bring about changes within the state either by peaceful means or, when peaceful means fail, by the use of force, by armed revolution. However, these statements in the proposed definitions coupled with the words of certain delegates before the committee imply something more. A recognition of a right to use force in the exercise of self-determination and a condemnation of the use of force to prevent such exercise might make illegal a use of force to put down the movement for self-determination either by outside states or by the metropolitan authority itself. Indeed, the metropolitan power or the government of the state wherein the movement for self-determination existed would be considered by some of the representatives as an external power and as an aggressor if it attempted to maintain its domination over the dependent dissident peoples by military force. If the state subjected to the break-away movement becomes an aggressor in its use of force against the movement, then it might well be deduced that another state acting to help the rebels by subversive methods would in reality not be acting as an aggressor but exercising the right of collective self-defense under Article 51 of the United Nations Charter.

To make types of subversion against a state illegal when taken for one purpose, say to overthrow the government of the state and substitute another in its place, and not illegal when they are undertaken on behalf of a liberation movement in a state would seem to be a departure from a general rule of law for a political, not a legal, reason. Moreover, it would be a dangerous rule if the principle of jurisdiction of a state over its territory and its people is to be maintained,[49] and further it would be extremely difficult to apply, for it would be almost impossible to say who are "dependent people." Any dissident group within a state could be considered a dependent people, and, if it is attempting to exercise what it claims to be a right of self-determination under this dubious doctrine, the attempt by the state to prevent it from doing so is illegal and the aid furnished the group by other states may no longer be considered internal aggression, but must be considered a legitimate action.

The Organization of American States has been the international body most concerned with the problem of subversion, particularly extracontinental subversion at the behest of totalitarian regimes.[50] During World War II, the inter-American system adopted a series of resolutions equating subversive activities with "political aggression" or "aggression of a non-military character." Stress was laid upon acts of espionage, sabotage, and surreptitious incitement, as well as subversive propaganda, as subversion and political aggression.[51]

At the Tenth Inter-American Conference in 1954, when concern was felt that Guatemala was coming under the domination of international communism, subversion was defined as the performance of acts directed, assisted, or instigated by foreign powers or government, constituting grave acts against the public order and security of the state, especially when the agent carrying out the subversive action is a national or citizen of the state subjected to the subversion.[52]

The statutes of the Inter-American Special Consultative Committee on Security, in 1963, defined communist subversive action as

any act of aggression or subversion or other act that may endanger the internal security of the American republics and the political defense of the hemisphere as well as the preparation of such acts that may arise from the continued intervention of the Sino-Soviet bloc in this hemisphere.[53]

In the same year this special committee pointed out that the Cuban regime of Fidel Castro had "begun a new phase of promoting and encouraging violent subversion in other countries of the hemisphere."[54] The committee named Venezuela as the primary target of this violent subversion which was supported by terror, sabotage, and guerrilla action. Thereafter the Organ of Consultation of the Organization of American States proclaimed that the government of Cuba openly intended to subvert Venezuelan institutions and overthrow its government. And it was clearly stated that such actions constituted aggression against Venezuela.[55]

The Organization of American States has clearly recognized that the concept of aggression includes modern subversive activities, and it may be noted that the OAS did not deign to use the adjective "indirect" when equating subversion with aggression.

In United Nations debates few or no attempts have been made to arrive at a definition of subversion or subversive activities. Discussion has been limited for the most part to the issue of whether or not subversion qualifies as aggression. The Essentials for Peace Resolution adopted by the General Assembly in 1949 called upon states "to refrain from any threat or acts, direct or indirect aimed at . . . subverting the will of the people in any state."[56] This resolution did not indicate what acts "subverting the will" might encompass, or whether such subverting of the will would be considered as aggression.

With reference to the Greek question, a United Nations Commission of Investigation placed a duty on Greece's northern neighbors to prevent and suppress subversive activity on their territory aimed against the Greek government.[57] This indicated that subversive activity or failure by a state to prevent or suppress such activity may be unlawful.

Under the 1954 Soviet definition of aggression, subversive activity was included in the concept of indirect aggression. Subversive activity was defined as "acts of terrorism, diversionary acts, etc." But acts generally thought to be subversionary, such as the fomentation of civil strife and internal upheaval in another state, were not included by the Russians within their meaning of subversive activity, although their promotion was said, along with subversion, to be indirect aggression.[58]

Some statesmen have objected to the application of the term *aggression* (direct or indirect) to an act of subversion, declaring that aggression involves an illegal use of force against which the state subjected to the aggression can react with a use of armed force. Thus certain drafts presented during the 1968 and 1969 attempts to define aggression would exclude subversive acts from the definition of aggression and at the same time limit by express language the right of a state victim in its own territory "of subversive and/or terrorist acts by irregular, volunteer or armed bands organized or supported by another State . . ." to have recourse to individual or collective self-defense against the delinquent state.[59] Others, claiming that an act of aggression consists of armed attack only, which may be met by resort to force in self-defense by the victim state, would subdivide the concept of subversion into subversive activities with an element of the use of force and subversive activities which do not involve such an element. Only the first would be included in the definition of aggression: "Subversion that involved the use of armed force would be covered automatically; to include subversion that did not, would widen the notion of aggression beyond the point of applicability and would thus do more harm than good."[60] The victim of unarmed subversive activities cannot then resort to armed force, but can only bring the issue to the United Nations for peaceful settlement.

Today, the term *subversion* designates all illegal activities, whether direct or indirect, overt or covert, conducted under the auspices of the authorities of a state and designed to overthrow the established government or vitally disrupt the public order of another state. Subversion combines psychological, political, social, and economic actions, as well as active military or paramilitary operations, and it is generally a sustained, long-run, intermeshed, and coordinated process. Consequently, it is usually impossible to place acts of subversion into neat little categorical definitions. Subversion, being a technique of opportunity, is successful mainly in areas where social and political revolution is at least incipient.[61] Where social or political disaffection is minimal, a nation may be irritated by subversion but can generally control its effects internally without appealing for international aid or resorting to international measures of self-help. Hence, to divide subversion into armed or unarmed activities is only to add confusion to the issue, for any serious type of illegal subversive activity carried on by the authorities of one state against another state ought to be considered aggression.

From any pragmatic point of view, no target state whose national independence was being destroyed by subversive activities would be willing to distinguish its retaliatory rights on the basis of whether the subversive activities consisted of the undertaking or encouragement of revolutionary activities by another state against it; or the toleration of organized activities to foment civil strife prior to an actual armed attack by the third party groups, even if no attack actually occurs; or the supplying of arms, money or other forms of aid to revolutionary groups or other armed bands; or the toleration of the use of another state's territory by individuals who are gathering together for purposes of civil strife against it; or the maintenance of fifth column activities in the state; or hostile propaganda for the fomentation of rebellion against its government. Subversive activities permitted or carried on by a state are illegal at international law, as intervention, and when they seriously endanger the rights of another state, its security and political independence, they are aggression. When carried out by a state surreptitiously and vicariously through third parties, they could be called indirect aggression, as could direct fomentation by a state of internal difficulties in another, particularly through propaganda media. But it would seem more advantageous to recognize that all subversion falls within the broader connotation of aggression.

As we have noted, the Soviets in their 1954 definition would confine indirect aggression to the encouragement of subversive activity (which they call acts of terrorism and diversionary acts), the promotion of the fomenting of civil war, the promotion of an internal upheaval, or the promotion of a change of policy in favor of the aggressor state. No differentiation is made as to whether the subversion is carried out by the state directly, or indirectly through intermediaries. Subversive activity is narrowly defined and apparently would not include promotion of the fomenting of civil war or internal upheaval, acts usually thought to be subversionary. The latter are of course included within the Russian concept of indirect aggression. Economic and ideological aggression are spoken of in separate contexts.[62] It is interesting to observe the changed Soviet position in 1969, for the draft definition of that year would confine aggression to armed aggression, direct or indirect, and indirect aggression was said to be committed by a state

by sending armed bands, mercenaries, terrorists or saboteurs to the territory of another State and engagement in other forms of subversive activity involving the use of armed force with the aim of promoting an internal upheaval in another State or a reversal of policy in favour of the aggressor.[63]

The Organization of American States has not been so timorous and has clearly characterized acts of subversion as aggression whether these acts are armed or not. Thus acts of hostile propaganda, terrorism, sabotage, and guerrilla warfare sponsored and directed by a state to overthrow the government of another state as well as the providing of funds, arms, and training in sabotage and guerrilla warfare to groups seeking to subvert national institutions have been designated as aggression pure and simple.[64] This was well brought out in 1963 when the government of Venezuela accused the government of Cuba of acts of intervention and aggression against the territorial integrity and sovereignty of Venezuela and sought the aid of the Organization of American States. An investigating committee found that Cuba had been guilty of acts falling within the following categories:

a. A hostile and systematic campaign of propaganda against the Government of Venezuela, as well as incitement to and support of the Communist subversion that is being carried out in that country;
b. Training in all kinds of subversive activities, of numerous Venezuelan citizens who traveled to Cuba for that purpose;
c. Remittance of funds through these travelers and other channels, for the purpose of maintaining and increasing subversive activities, and
d. The provision of arms to guerrilla and terrorist groups operating in Venezuela.[65]

The committee concluded that Venezuela had been a target of actions sponsored and directed by the government of Cuba which were intended to subvert Venezuelan institutions and overthrow that nation's democratic government through terror, sabotage, assault, and guerrilla warfare. This Cuban support of subversion was called political aggression.[66]

Upon receiving the report of the investigating committee, the Ninth Meeting of Consultation declared that the acts verified by the committee constituted an aggression and intervention on the part of the government of Cuba in the internal affairs of Venezuela, an aggression which affected all of the member states. It emphatically condemned the government of Cuba and, in accordance with the provisions of Articles 6 and 8 of the Rio Treaty, called upon all members to sever diplomatic and consular relations with Cuba, suspend all trade except in foodstuffs, medicines, and medical equipment, and suspend all sea transportation between themselves and Cuba with the exception of that necessary for humanitarian reasons.

Cuba was also warned that if it should persist in carrying out aggressive and subversive acts, the member states intended to "preserve their essential rights as sovereign states by the use of self-defense in either individual or collective form which could go as far as resort to armed force, until such times as the Organ of Consultation takes measures to guarantee the peace and security of the hemisphere."[67]

Consequently, it can be seen that the inter-American system has recognized that insofar as this hemisphere is concerned the concept of aggression includes a host of modern subversive techniques.

IDEOLOGICAL AGGRESSION

Inasmuch as international law recognizes that each independent and sovereign state is accorded the right to shape its cultural, social, economic, and political life as it wishes,[68] a foreign intrusion by another state which imposes or attempts to impose a certain philosophical pattern within this area can fall within the meaning of ideological aggression.[69] The definition of ideological aggression as an imposition of an ideology describes its meaning in relation to the end or objective which is sought. Discussion of this phenomenon by authorities tends, however, to center around the means or methods by which this type of aggression is effectuated, although there is manifest agreement that the end-objective of these methods is the actual or intended imposition of an ideology. The term *ideological* pertains to ideology, and since ideology signifies the science of ideas of the understanding, of mental philosophy, the means used to carry out ideological aggression are those adapted to the molding of the thought processes of the people of a state so as to maintain the condition of things in the state intact or to effect a change in the condition of things in that state so as to accord with the aggressor's wishes. Ideological aggression, then, is the spreading of ideas intentionally and deliberately so as to manipulate by symbols controversial attitudes and positions.[70] It is hostile propaganda indulged in by a state directly or vicariously to incite and influence the people of another state so as to maintain or alter the institutions and policies of that state. The campaign of hostile propaganda may emanate from within or without the territory of the victim state and can be carried on by any means of communications.[71]

Hostile propaganda falls into three categories.[72] The first, war-mongering propaganda, is described as follows:

Direct public propaganda urging the state to be the first to commit, contrary to its international understandings, any one of the following acts: a) declaration of war upon another state; b) invasion by its armed forces, even without declaration of war, of the territory of another state; c) attack by its land, naval or air forces, even without declaration of war, upon the territory, vessels or aircraft of another state; d) naval blockade of the coasts or ports of another state; e) assistance, given to armed bands, organized in its territory which have invaded the territory of another state, or refusal, in spite of the request of the invaded state, to take in its territory all possible steps to deprive the aforesaid bands of all assistance or protection.[73]

From this quotation it can be seen that war-mongering propaganda occurs in time of peace and does not include propaganda in wartime. If, however, the aim of war-mongering propaganda is successful, it will lead to a state of international war.

The second type of propaganda is called subversive. The purpose is not the promotion of international war, but rather the promotion of civil strife or civil war within a state so as to topple the existing institutional structure of the state and bring about a change in the existing regime.[74] Such subversive propaganda is directed to the creation of doubt and distrust in the minds of the people of the state concerning their institutions so that uprising will occur to effectuate change. Inasmuch as the principle of sovereignty and political independence gives to each state the right freely to choose its own form of government, subversive propaganda carried on by another state which attempts overtly to incite acts of rebellion or covertly to gain control of the government by infiltration or by the sowing of erosive attitudes against existing structures can be considered as ideological aggression.[75]

The third type of ideological aggression, defamatory propaganda, is directed against the leaders of the government of a state. Its objective is to expose such leaders to obloquy and opprobrium so as to dishonor them in the minds of their fellow countrymen and thereby to bring about their downfall.

Defamatory propaganda violates customary international law.[76] At first it was considered to be a detraction from the right of respect which one state owed to another,[77] but as early as 1816 some writers were aware defamatory propaganda could be resorted to in order "to render the people of that country discontented with their government, and to excite them to attempt its subversion."[78] It has, therefore, been accepted that such propaganda is an intervention into domestic affairs of a state, subversive in nature, which seeks to undermine the government or institutions of that state by turning the populace against its rulers. It is a policy of inducing serious civil disturbance in other states, and, as aggression, has been met with various sanctions, such as breach of diplomatic relations. Consider the following language:

Thus the Cuban Foreign Minister has applied unprintable language to President Frondizi of Argentina. Government broadcasts have denounced President Lopez Matéos as "the betrayer of the Mexican Revolution," President Alessandri as "the corrupter of the faith of the Chilean people," President Lleras Camargo of Colombia as "the intimate friend of exploiting imperialism," President Betan-. court of Venezuela as the "revolutionary of Mercurochrome Bandaids," President Eisenhower of the United States as "decrepit" and "bottle-fed." . . . In consequence . . . several American states no longer have diplomatic relations with Cuba.[78]

Hostile propaganda in all three forms has been included in charges of subversive activities made before international organizations. For example, the Security Council in 1958 had before it a Lebanese complaint[80] which charged the United Arab Republic with internal interferences in Lebanon by the infiltration of armed bands, by engaging in terrorist activities, and by the waging of a propaganda campaign through the press and radio calling for strikes and demonstrations in Lebanon and for the overthrow of Lebanese authorities. The United Arab Republic answered saying that the use of news media could not affect peace and security, and further that such media were being used to defend against Lebanese attacks against the United Arab Republic by the same method. A resolution demanding that noninterference be "maintained by word and deed" was ultimately forthcoming from the General Assembly.[81] A flagrant aggression by the government of North Viet Nam against Laos by the training and arming of troops to engage in guerrilla warfare, and by the use of the Hanoi radio to incite Laotians to revolt, was a subject of charges in 1959.[82] The investigating committee for the Security Council found that certain North Vietnamese conduct was being directed against Laos, but did not decide whether such conduct was illegal.[83]

Haiti came before the Organization of American States in 1949, calling attention to acts of the Dominican Republic which were said to create a situation that might endanger the peace and which were characterized as a "moral aggression."[84] The Dominican acts consisted of the broadcast of a speech over the government-owned Dominican radio by an exiled Haitian which was "of an extremely vulgar and provocative nature insulting to the President of the Republic of Haiti."[85] The Dominican government declared that the radio station was not official but private, and that all it had done was to grant political asylum to a Haitian and to permit him to deliver certain talks on a private broadcasting station which, though possibly of a disagreeable chararcter, were his own responsibility. After reviewing the case the Council concluded that the defamatory propaganda had not yet reached a stage where it could be considered as affecting the political independence of Haiti so as to require a consultative meeting. The Council could hardly have been impressed by the Dominican statement to the effect that it was only private propaganda activity, in view of the tightly controlled dictatorship existing in the Dominican Republic at that time. Propaganda of a defamatory nature carried on under such control cannot be classified as private and therefore devoid of state responsibility.[86]

In November, 1961, the Inter-American Peace Committee conducted a study of the subversive activities emanating from the communist government of Cuba against other American republics.[87] On the basis of the evidence it gathered, the committee reported:

There exists a constant and systematic activity of radio propaganda through the government transmitters of Cuba, aimed at defaming the governments of other countries of the Hemisphere, discrediting representative democratic institutions, insulting the executives of other republics of the Hemisphere, fomenting public disorders, and even inciting violent subversion of the legally constituted regimes. The government press and that of the single party of the Cuban government also constantly carry on work along the same line.[88]

It was concluded that such activities were acts of "political aggression," "aggression of a nonmilitary character," representing attacks upon inter-American peace and security as well as upon the sovereignty and political independence of the American states and therefore a serious violation of fundamental principles of the inter-American system. When the report was presented to the Eighth Meeting of Consultation of Ministers of Foreign Affairs, the meeting determined that because of such activities the present government of Cuba had excluded itself from the inter-American system. Its subversive activities, including defamatory propaganda, were so incompatible with the principles of the inter-American system that the government of Cuba had placed itself outside the OAS.[89]

A Special Consultative Committee on Security, composed of experts on security matters, with the duty to make recommendations in the field of security against the subversive action of international communism, was also established by the Eighth Meeting.[90] This committee has since its inception cautioned the American nations of the increasingly intense subversive campaign being carried out by Cuba against the Western Hemisphere nations. This subversive campaign employs terrorism, sabotage, infiltration into governments, and all types of hostile propaganda campaigns. In a study prepared for the Second Special Inter-American Conference, the Special Consultative Committee on Security stated:

It is necessary and urgent, for the purpose of adequately defending democracy:
a. That the intervention of communism in the internal affairs of the American Republics be considered as aggression, since it constitutes a threat to the security of the hemisphere.[91]

Cuban subversion did not cease, however, and at the end of 1963 Venezuela accused the government of Cuba of acts of intervention and aggression.[92] The denunciation set forth an aggregate of acts which violated the sovereignty and political independence of Venezuela and which at the same time were contrary to the most fundamental principles of the inter-American system. These acts included a hostile and systematic campaign of propaganda against the Venezuelan government, as well as incitement to and support of the communist subversion that was being carried out in that country. The Council of the OAS called the Ninth Meeting of Consultation of Ministers of Foreign Affairs to deal with this complaint. The investigating committee found that programs were transmitted daily by Radio Havana intended for Venezuela, instigating terrorist and guerrilla activities, instructing leaders of the Venezuelan Communist Party in ways to foment civil strife, inviting Venezuelan leftists to address their compatriots over Radio Havana to incite them to rebellion and to exhort them to support the leftists' "revolutionary" action, and unendingly haranguing the Venezuelan people, urging them to overthrow the government.[93] The committee also found books, pamphlets, magazines, newspapers, and other publications of a subversive nature which had been published in Cuba, and which had been confiscated from persons belonging to terrorist groups, guerrilla movements, or communist front organizations.

The Ninth Meeting of Consultation of Ministers of Foreign Affairs, serving as Organ of Consultation in the application of the Rio Treaty, concluded that Venezuela had been the victim of a series of actions sponsored and directed by the government of Cuba, openly intended to subvert Venezuelan institutions and to overthrow the democratic government of Venezuela through terrorism, sabotage, assault, hostile propaganda, and guerrilla warfare. All of these acts were said to constitute intervention and aggression and to be in conflict with the principles and aims of the inter-American system.[94] The meeting condemned the government of Cuba for such acts and called for a collective rupture by the American Republics of diplomatic and consular relations with that government, for the suspension of trade with Cuba except in foodstuffs and medicines, and for the suspension of sea transportation between the American republics and Cuba except for reasons of a humanitarian nature.[95]

On March 7, 1966, the government of Ghana protested before the Organization of African Unity[96] of acts of aggression and intervention in the internal affairs of Ghana by the government of Guinea. Ghana pointed out that on October 24, 1965,[97] the Organization of African Unity had set forth a Declaration on Subversion by which all member states agreed not to tolerate the use of their territory for any subversive activities against another member state, and agreed to refrain from conducting any press or radio campaigns against another member state. The acts complained of by Ghana were those permitting the deposed former dictator of Ghana to broadcast over the government radio facilities of Guinea threats to the lives of members of the government and armed forces of Ghana, calls for revolt, and demands for the initiation of terrorist campaigns. Ghana declared that it would use all necessary measures to protect itself from such subversive activities on the part of the government of Guinea.

A hostile propaganda attack carried on by one state against another of such a magnitude as to endanger the security of the state against which it is directed can be classified as aggression—as ideological aggression.[98] It is nothing short of an attack against the international personality of a state. Inasmuch as it does not involve the use of armed force it can qualify as indirect aggression, although it would seem to make for greater clarity to label it simply as aggression.[99] To fall within the category of aggression it must in general be directed by a state against another state. It is states (and in some instances other entities) which are precluded from spreading hostile propaganda against or within other states.

Vattel asserted that "the nation, or the sovereign, must not allow its citizens to injure the subjects of another State, much less to offend the State itself,"[100] and his view was accepted by certain other publicists who declared that the mere toleration of private propaganda against friendly states was a violation of international law.[101] However, the weight of authority would hold otherwise, to the effect that while states themselves are obligated under international law not to engage in hostile propaganda, they have no duty to prevent private persons from doing so.

The rule of no responsibility for private hostile propaganda was derived from various sources. The press, for example, has long been considered as a private and independent institution, and is generally free from governmental control in nontotalitarian nations. Such nations believe strongly in freedom of the press and freedom of speech, despite the fact that such freedoms might have some incidental ill effects on international affairs. Moreover, the belief is that free expression will in the long run lead to international peace and understanding more than would censorship. Second, as some types of subversive propaganda come from refugees who have been given asylum for a political offense against their government, most liberal and democratic governments feel a strong antipathy against inhibiting such refugees' rights of free speech and expression.

Although it is established that state responsibility does not ensue from private propaganda activities against another state, the rule is not absolute. Private propaganda is carried on by all the modern communications media: books, press and publications, radio, television, and films. Books, press and publications, and films are regulated completely only in totalitarian nations, but radio and television are under some measure of state control in every country, whether or not they are privately owned. From this state control through licensing and assignment of wavelengths certain writers would deduce that there is an obligation on states to use due diligence to see that in international programs the radio or television station is not used as a means of spreading hostile propaganda in another country.[102]

There is one well-established exception to the rule that states are not responsible for private subversive propaganda, and that is if the private subversive propaganda takes the form of terroristic incitement. If private propaganda urges assassination, sabotage, or other acts of terror, it is no longer privileged and states are required to use all reasonable means to suppress it. Terroristic incitement is a crime against the peace and security of mankind.[103]

ECONOMIC AGGRESSION

Economic aggression can be used as a tool to subjugate one nation to the will of another. By this method a people can be put into a position of economic adversity which can lead to internal strife and ultimately can possibly result in loss of state independence. Dr. Garcia-Amador, the former Cuban representative in the General Assembly's Sixth Committee, set forth its significance clearly when in 1949 he stated:

Economic aggression could assume many forms, ranging from threats of, or the effective application of, enforcement measures intended to obtain or maintain advantages or specific situations, to the suppression of free competition in the international market and the economic subjugation of the country which was the victim of that kind of aggression. In all those cases, it was the economic integrity and independence of the State which were undermined and even completely destroyed. All States were vulnerable to that type of aggression, but those it affected most were the countries with the least developed or the least diversified economy, because an attack upon one of their basic products could upset their entire economic structure.[104]

Because the economies of most of the Latin American countries are little diversified, the inter-American system began as early as 1938, in its conferences, to concern itself with the problem.[105] It was the subject of much discussion at the Ninth Inter-American Conference in 1948. Inasmuch as it was emphasized by the Cuban delegate, it was called *Doctrina Grau* after the President of Cuba, Ramon Grau San Martín. The Cuban proposal would proscribe unilateral coercive measures of an economic, financial, or commercial character until all peaceful procedures had been exhausted.[106] The notion was finally broadened to include types of activities other than economic and was included in Article 16 of the Charter of the Organization of American States. The wording of the provision was, "No State may use or encourage the use of coercive measures of an economic or political character in order to force the sovereign will of another State and obtain from it advantages of any kind."[107]

Although a state at international law may chart its own economic course in its relations with other states,[108] still all states are restricted by the rule that a policy cannot be exercised for the sole purpose of causing injury to and forcing the will of another state unless such economic coercion is used in the exercise of the right of self-defense or reprisal. An illegal intervention[109] of an economic nature becomes aggression if it jeopardizes essential rights of a state which are requisite to its security.

Economic aggression in this sense would take its meaning from the method employed. Economic means are used to effectuate the aggression. The inter-American principle as well as the 1965 non-intervention resolution of the General Assembly of the United Nations follows such a meaning by prohibiting *measures of an economic and compelling character* to force the will of a state.[110] The manipulation of tariffs, the imposition of embargoes and boycotts, the freezing of funds, etc.[111] can all be employed in such a way as to constitute economic aggression.

In defining economic aggression some authorities speak not of the measures used, but of the purpose or object of the aggression. If the purpose or objective of the aggressor state is to gain economic benefits from the nation, or to dispossess it of economic resources, economic aggression is thought to exist. The methods used to coerce, whether they be armed, diplomatic, or economic, are unimportant. Bolivia, in a draft definition of 1952, looked upon economic aggression from this point of view. It defined economic aggression as a "unilateral action to deprive a State of the economic resources derived from the fair practice of international trade, or to endanger its basic economy, thus jeopardizing the security of that State."[112] It has also been defined as conduct which takes from a state its essential resources or interferes with the normal condition of its economy, internal or international.[113]

As of 1954 the Soviet Union combined the two ideas by declaring that economic aggression occurs when a state first commits the following acts:

(a) Takes against another State measures of economic pressure violating its sovereignty and economic independence and threatening the bases of its economic life;
(b) Takes against another State measures preventing it from exploiting or nationalizing its own national riches;
(c) Subjects another State to an economic blockade.[114]

Under (a) economic aggression would exist because economic measures of coercion were employed. It should be noted, however, that such measures must be taken to carry out an economic objective within the victim state, inasmuch as such economic measures must violate the victim's "economic independence and threaten the basis of its economic life."

Section (b) concerns itself solely with the economic objective, as does

Section (c). An economic blockade is one instituted for an economic purpose, i.e., to take from the state its economic resources. Such a blockade would be effectuated by the use of armed force. If illegal, it would be designated as an armed aggression. The employment of economic measures as measures of illegal coercion would seem to define economic aggression more closely than would a definition directed to an economic objective. Perhaps the definition should include and combine both meanings, i.e., illegal economic measures employed by a state against another state so as to force the sovereign will of the latter and to deprive it of economic resources or disturb its economic life, thereby jeopardizing its security.

There has been resistance to and criticism of any inclusion of economic coercion within the meaning of aggression. Among those who have demurred have been not only those United Nations delegates who felt that the meaning of aggression should not be expanded beyond armed attack, but also representatives who felt that such an extension of aggression's meaning would be so unlimited that it would give the Security Council complete discretion in a multitude of cases not involving force.[115] Some doubts might be allayed if economic aggression were defined as something more than illegal intervention. It must be conduct so grave as to affect the security of a state and thus to threaten international peace and security. This would set forth a test for reaction by the international community.

NOTES

CHAPTER ONE

1. Resolution 2330 (XXII), December 18, 1967, as contained in Report of the Special Committee on the Question of Defining Aggression, U.N. GAOR, 23rd Sess., Agenda Item 86, A/7185/Rev. 1. See also 5 U.N. Monthly Chronicle 34-41 (No. 1, Jan. 1968). For discussion of the renewed U.N. consideration see J. Hazard, "Why Try Again To Define Aggression?" 62 Am. J. Int. L. 701 (1968).

2. See *infra*, chap. 2.

3. See Report of the Special Committee on the Question of Defining Aggression, *supra* note 1, at 13-18.

4. *Id.* at 13, 18.

5. 5 U.N. Monthly Chronicle 4 (No. 8, Aug.-Sept. 1968).

6. See A. J. Thomas, Jr. and A. V. W. Thomas, The Organization of American States 316-37 (1963); Report of the Special Committee on the Question of Defining Aggression, *supra* note 1, at 14, 18; Case between Venezuela and Cuba 1963-1964, 2 P.A.U., Inter-American Treaty of Reciprocal Assistance Applications 181 *et seq.* (1964).

7. See A. J. Thomas, Jr. and A. V. W. Thomas, The Dominican Republic Crisis 1965, The Working Paper (The Hammarskjöld Forums 1967).

8. Report of the Special Committee on the Question of Defining Aggression, *supra* note 1, at 15-18.

9. Remarks of the representative of the U.K. before the Committee on Defining Aggression in April, 1967 as set forth in 4 U.N. Monthly Chronicle 55 (No. 5, May 1967); remarks of the representatives of Australia, China, Thailand before the General Assembly in December, 1967 as set forth in 5 U.N. Monthly Chronicle 36, 39 (No. 1, Jan. 1968).

10. B. Röling, "On Aggression, on International Criminal Law, on International Criminal Jurisdiction," 2 Nederlands Tijdschrift voor International Recht 167 at 174 (1955).

11. See remarks of the representatives of Norway and Thailand, 5 U.N. Monthly Chronicle 37, 39 (No. 1, 1968).

12. See D. Sidjanski and S. Castanos, " 'L'Agresseur' et 'l'Agression' au Point de Vue Ideologique et Real," 30 Revue de Droit International 44 at 45 (1952); J. Stone, Aggression and World Order 112 (1958).

13. 6 The Collected Papers of John Bassett Moore 444 (1944).

14. The Soviet Union's perambulations in this regard are suggestive of a politically-directed course. For discussion of some of these perambulations see B. Ramundo and A. Rusis, The Socialist Theory of International Law 2 (1964); J. Hazard, Law and Social Change in the U.S.S.R. 70, 293 (1953); A. Bouscaren, Soviet Foreign Policy: A Pattern of Persistence 134-38 (1962); J. Schulz, "Der Sowjetsche Begriff der Aggression," 2 Osteuropa-Recht 274, 284 (1956); see Report of the Special Committee on the Question of the Definition of Aggression, *supra* note 1, at 14, 17-18.

15. See Hazard, *supra* note 1, at 703-5.

16. G. Fitzmaurice, "Inter Arma Silent Definitiones," 3 Sydney L. Rev. 71 (1959).

17. J. Brierly, The Outlook for International Law 45 (1944).

18. P. Spaak, "The West in Disarray," 35 Foreign Affairs 184 (1956); E. Aroneanu, La Définition de l'Agression: Exposé Objectif 200-201 (1958).

19. C. Chacko, "International Law and the Concept of Aggression," 3 Indian J. Int. L. 396 (1963).

20. L. Podesta Costa, 2 Derecho Internacional Publico 147 (1955); C. Urrutia

Aparicio, "La Revolución del Concepto de la Agresión en el Derecho Internacional," 1 Revista de la Asociación Guatemalteca de Derecho Internacional 80 at 89 (1954).

21. B. Murty, "Aggression in International Law," 7 India Quarterly 27 (Jan.-March 1951).

22. For a discussion on the techniques of definition see H. Hart, "Definition and Theory in Jurisprudence," 1954 L. Q. Rev. 37 *et seq.*

23. Aroneanu, *supra* note 18, at 187-90.

24. G. Fitzmaurice, "The Definition of Aggression," 1 Int. and Comp. L. Q. 137 (1952).

25. Remarks of the representative of the U.S. before the Committee on Defining Aggression as contained in 4 U.N. Monthly Chronicle 52 (No. 5, May 1937).

26. Stone, *supra* note 12, at 77.

27. Yearbook of the International Law Commission 1951, p. 69; Aroneanu, *supra* note 18 at 200-201.

28. See *infra* pp. 14-15.

29. A. Spiropoulos, "La Question de la Définition de l'Agression devant les Nations Unies," in Mélange en l'Honneur de Gilbert Gidel 543 at 549 (1961); R. Pal, "What Is Aggressive War?" 4 Indian L. Rev. 105 (1950).

30. The Inter-American Treaty of Reciprocal Assistance is contained in Thomas and Thomas, *supra* note 6, at 429 *et seq.* For discussion see *id.* at 267-68.

31. H. Kelsen, "E Possible e Desiderabile Definire l'Aggressione," in Scritti de Diritto Internazionale in Onore de Tomaso Perassi 13 (1957); B. Supervielle, "Las Nuevas Formas de Agresión," 11 Revista de la Facultad de Derecho y Ciencias Sociales de Montevideo 435 (1960); C. Chaumont, "Explication Juridique d'Une Définition de l'Agression," 2 Annuaire Français de Droit International 521 (1956).

32. Stone, *supra* note 12, at 74-77.

33. G. Fitzmaurice, "The Definition of Aggression," 1 Int. & Comp. L. Q. 137 (1952); Note, "Meaning of 'Aggression' in the United Nations Charter," 33 Neb. L. Rev. 606 (1954).

34. B. Röling, "The Question of Defining Aggression," in Symbolae Verzijl 324 (1958); C. Mahoney, "The Problem of Defining Aggression," 31 Dept. State Bull. 872 (1954).

35. I. Brownlie, International Law and the Use of Force by States 355 (1963); H. Kelsen, Collective Security under International Law (U.S. Naval War College International Law Studies) 66-85 (1961).

36. M. McDougal and F. Feliciano, Law and Minimum World Public Order 62 (1961).

37. L. Sohn, "The Definition of Aggression," 45 Va. L. Rev. 697 (1959).

38. *Id.* at 698.

39. *Id.*

40. Kelsen, *supra* note 35, at 73.

41. R. Alfaro, "La Question de la Définition de l'Agression," 29 Revue de droit international, de sciences diplomatiques, politiques et sociales 367 (ed. Sottile, 1951).

42. S. Glaser, "Constituye un Crimen la Guerra de Agresion?" 6 Revista Española de Derecho Internacional 539 (1953).

43. M. Borquin, Collective Security 329 (1936); B. Braatoy, "The Quest for Treaty Definitions of Aggression," 5 Acta Scandinavica Juris Gentium 29 (1934).

44. Aroneanu, *supra* note 18, at 141.

45. C. H. M. Waldock, "The Regulation of the Use of Force by Individual States in International Law," 81 Recueil des Cours 455 at 506-11.

46. Spiropoulos, *supra* note 29, at 547.

47. 1951 Yearbook of the United Nations 833 (1952).

48. Kelsen, *supra* note 35, at 70.

49. L. Kopelmanas, "The Problem of Aggression and Prevention of War," 31 Am. J. Int. L. 244 (1937).

50. L. Kotzsch, The Concept of War in Contemporary History and International Law 76, 82 (1956).

51. Kelsen, *supra* note 35, at 74.

CHAPTER TWO

1. For bibliographies of studies on aggression see L. Sohn, Cases and Other Materials on World Law 801-6 (1950); 6 M. Hudson, International Legislation 411 (1937). For later works see J. Stone, Aggression and World Order (1958); E. Aroneanu, La Définition de l'Agression (1958); W. Komarnicki, "De la Définition de l'Agresseur," 75 Recueil de Cours 5 (1949); C. Pompe, Aggressive War an International Crime (1953).

2. C. Lewis and C. Short, A Latin Dictionary 71 (Imp. 1958).

3. See *infra* pp. 57-65.

4. 4 A. Bustamante, Derecho Internacional Publico 160 (1937).

5. See *infra* pp. 50-51.

6. The Classics of International Law, 2 Selections from Three Works of Francisco Suárez 803-4 (Scott ed. 1944).

7. E. de Vattel, The Law of Nations or Principles of the Law of Nature 302 (Chitty ed. 1876).

8. See Pompe, *supra* note 1, at 46-52.

9. For discussion see C. Eagleton, "The Attempt to Define Aggression," International Conciliation No. 264 (1930).

10. Art. 231, Treaty of Versailles, III T.I.A.S. 3331 at 3419 (1923).

11. Eagleton, *supra* note 9, at 589.

12. Art. 11 Covenant of the League of Nations, III T.I.A.S. 3339 (1923).

13. For discussion see Eagleton, *supra* note 9, at 591-94.

14. L.N.O.J. Spec. Supp. No. 16 (1923) Annex 10 (Pt. I) pp. 203-9.

15. *Id.* at 183-85.

16. Eagleton, *supra* note 9, states at p. 596 that "the lack of an acceptable definition of aggression was recognized by all States as the chief defect of the treaty."

17. The Protocol for the Pacific Settlement of International Disputes is contained in 2 M. Hudson, International Legislation 1378 (1931). The protocol was never ratified. For discussion of its terms see Miller, The Geneval Protocol (1925).

18. Treaty of Mutual Guarantee, Locarno. The text is contained in 3 Hudson, International Legislation 1689 (1931). For other resolutions see G. von Glahn, Law among Nations 518-19 (2d ed. 1970).

19. Treaty for the Renunciation of War. Text in 4 Hudson, *id.* at 2522.

20. As set forth in D. Myers, "Origin and Conclusion of the Paris Pact," World Peace Foundation Pamphlets Vol. 12, No. 2, p. 167 at 170 (1929).

21. See Wolfers, Discord and Collaboration, Essays on International Politics 254 (1962).

22. This text is contained in Report by the Secretary General, 7 U.N. GAOR, Annex, Agenda Item 54 at 34-35, U.N. Doc. A/2211 (1952).

23. *Id.*

24. *Id.* A protocol annexed to Article 22 of the act relating to the definition of the aggressor was favored by some of the parties. This protocol would declare that an act of aggression could not be justified by the internal condition or international conduct of a state, even though the latter violated or threatened violation of the material or moral rights or interests of a foreign state or its nationals, by a rupture of diplomatic or economic relations, by an economic or financial boycott, by a dispute relating to economic, financial, or other obligations toward foreign states, or finally by a frontier incident. *Id.* at 35.

25. 6 Hudson, International Legislation 410 (1937).

26. *Id.*

27. L.N.O.J. Spec. Supp. No. 112, Records of the Special Session of the Assembly, vol. 4 (1933) pp. 22, 72, 75.

28. Dispute between Bolivia and Paraguay, Records of the Special Session of the Assembly, L. N.O.J. Spec. Supp. No. 132 (1934) p. 48.

29. L.N.O.J. 16th year, No. 11; Eighty-eighth Session of the Council (1935) p. 1225.

30. L.N.O.J. 20th year, No. 11-12 (Part II): One Hundred and Seventh Session of the Council, (1939) p. 506, (Doc. A. 46, 1939 VII).

31. International Conference on Military Trials, Report of Robert H. Jackson, Dept. State Pub. No. 3080 (1949).

32. *Id.* at 294.

33. *Id.* at 302-3, 308.

34. For summary of the Nuremberg proceedings see Pompe, *supra* note 1, chap. 4.

35. United Nations Conference on International Organization, Documents, vol. 6, p. 584 (1945).

36. *Id.* at 538.

37. *Id.*, vol. 12, p. 505.

38. Art. 39, U.N. Charter.

39. Art. 2(4), U.N. Charter.

40. Art. 51 U.N. Charter.

41. Arts. 42, 44, 45, 48, 49, U.N. Charter.

42. 5 U.N. GAOR First Comm. 247-49 (1950).

43. *Id.* at 256-57.

44. The Soviet Union's draft resolution is contained in 1950 Y.B.U.N. 210.

45. 5 U.N. GAOR First Committee, *supra* note 42, at 265, 277.

46. 1950 Y.B.U.N. 206-7.

47. *Id.* at 195.

48. For First Committee discussions see 5 U.N. GAOR First Committee 176-246 (1950).

49. 1950 Y.B.U.N. 200-204.

50. *Id.*

51. 1947-1948 Y.B.U.N. 214.

52. Text of the draft code is contained in 1951 Y.B. Int'l L. Comm'n, vol. II, pp. 134-37.

53. *Id.*, art. 2(1).

54. *Id.* art. 2(2).

55. *Id.* art. 2(4)(5)(6).

56. 1951 Y.B.U.N. 842.

57. 1951 Y. B. Int'l L. Comm'n, vol. II, p. 58.

58. *Id.*

59. *Id.* at 59-60.

60. *Id.* at 61.

61. *Id.* at 79-80.

62. See *supra* p. 23.

63. 1951 Y.B.U.N. 833.

64. *Id.* See also 1951 Y.B. Int'l L. Comm'n, vol. II, pp. 131-33.

65. 1954 Y.B. Int'l L. Comm'n, vol. II, 151-52.

66. *Id.* at vol. 1, 129.

67. *Id.* at 130.

68. *Id.*

69. *Id.* at 127.

70. *Id.* at 140.

71. *Id.*

72. *Id.* at 139.

73. *Id.* at 140.

74. *Id.*

75. *Id.* at 141.

76. *Id.*

77. *Id.*

78. *Id.*
79. *Id.*
80. *Id.*
81. *Id.* at 142.
82. *Id.* at 177.
83. *Id.* at 178.
84. *Id.* at 176.
85. 1954 Y.B.U.N. 208-10.
86. 1951 Y.B.U.N. 834-40.
87. *Id.* at 839.
88. See "The Question of Defining Aggression," 1952 Y.B.U.N. 784-91.
89. Report of the Special Committee on the Question of Defining Aggression, 9 U.N. GAOR, Supp. 11, U.N. Doc. 11(A/2638) (1954).
90. *Id.* at 7.
91. *Id.* at 7-10.
92. *Id.* at 8.
93. *Id.* at 7.
94. *Id.* at 6.
95. *Id.* at 7-8.
96. *Id.* at 7.
97. *Id.* at 8-10.
98. *Id.* at 8-9.
99. *Id.* at 9.
100. *Id.*
101. *Id.*
102. *Id.* at 9-10.
103. *Id.* at 10.
104. *Id.* at 12.
105. *Id.*
106. The Soviet draft is set forth *id.* at 13-14.
107. *Id.* at 14-15.
108. *Id.* at 14.
109. *Id.* at 15.
110. 9 U.N. GAOR, First Comm. 33 (1954).
111. For the debates see *id.* at 33-93.
112. 1954 Y.B.U.N. 429-30.
113. The drafts which were submitted are contained in Report of the 1956 Special Committee on the Question of Defining Aggression, 12 U.N. GAOR, Supp. 16, Doc. A/3574 (1957).
114. *Id.* at 7-8.
115. *Id.* at 15.
116. *Id.*
117. For texts of the drafts see the report *id.* at 16, 31-33.
118. For discussion of all of these points see the report, *id.* at 1-25.
119. 1957 Y.B.U.N. 371-74.
120. 1959 Y.B.U.N. 420.
121. 1962 Y.B.U.N. 506-7.
122. 1965 Y.B.U.N. 647.
123. For these proceedings see 4 U.N. Monthly Chronicle 51-58 (No. 5, May 1967); 4 U.N. Monthly Chronicle 79-81 (No. 6, June 1967); 5 U.N. Monthly Chronicle 35-41, 117-18 (No. 1, Jan. 1968).
124. For Report of the Special Committee on the Question of Defining Aggression see 23 U.N. GAOR, Agenda Item No. 86, U.N. Doc. A/7185/Rev. 1 (1967).
125. *Id.* at 4-5.
126. *Id.*
127. *Id.* at 5-6.
128. *Id.* at 22.

129. U.N. GAOR, 1968 Special Committee on the Question of Defining Aggression, Summary Records of the First to Twenty-Fourth Meetings, U.N. Doc. A/AC.134/-SR. 1-24 (Sept. 30, 1968) at pp. 54-55.

130. Arts. 3 and 7 of the twelve power and Latin American drafts respectively. See Report of the Special Committee, *supra* note 124, at 5 and 6.

131. U.N. GAOR, 1968 Special Committee, *supra* note 129, at 146.

132. *Id.* at 131, 165, 221.

133. For summaries of debates and criticisms on draft proposals see Report of the Special Committee, *supra* note 124, at 26-32.

134. For this draft see, *id.* at 7-8.

135. *Id.* at 9-10.

136. 23 U.N. GAOR, Annexes, Agenda Item No. 86 at 4-8, U.N. Doc. A/C.6/L. 734 (1968).

137. See Report of the Special Committee on the Question of Defining Aggression, 24 February-3 April 1969, 24 U.N. GAOR, Supp. No. 20, U.N. Doc. A/7620. For summary of the action of the Special Committee see 6 U.N. Monthly Chronicle 78-81 (No. 4, April 1969).

138. For this draft see Report of the Special Committee, *id.* at 8-9.

139. *Id.* at 13. For the Soviet draft see *id.* at 4-6.

140. *Id.* at 5.

141. *Id.* at 15.

142. *Id.* at 16.

143. *Id.* at 18.

144. *Id.* at 22, 30.

145. *Id.* at 8.

146. *Id.* at 17, 18, 26, 27.

147. *Id.* at 5, 7.

148. See A. J. Thomas, Jr. and A. V. W. Thomas, Legal Limits on the Use of Chemical and Biological Weapons chaps. 4 and 5, pp. 218-26 (1970).

149. *Id.*

150. This lack of preamble was regarded by some as a backward step. *Id.* at 25.

151. *Id.* at 8.

152. *Id.* at 9.

153. *Id.* at 27.

154. *Id.*

155. *Id.* at 32.

156. 7 U.N. Monthly Chronicle 174-75 (No. 1, Jan. 1970).

157. Report of the Secretary General on the work of the Organization—16 June 1970-15 June 1971, 26 U.N. GAOR Supp. No. 1 (A/8401) p. 235 (1971).

158. 25 U.N. GAOR Res. 2644 (XXV) Supp. No. 19 (A/8019) (1970).

159. Report of the Special Committee on the Question of Defining Aggression—1 February-5 March 1971, 26 U.N. GAOR Supp. No. 19 (A/8419) p. 3 (1971).

160. Report of the Secretary General *supra* note 157 at 236.

161. *Id.*

162. Report of the Special Committee *supra* note 159 at 30.

163. *Id.*

164. *Id.*

165. *Id.* at 31.

166. Report of the Secretary General *supra* note 157 at 236.

167. New York Times, December 9, 1971.

CHAPTER THREE

1. Article 39 of the UN Charter reads:

The Security Council shall determine the existence of any threat to the peace, breach of the peace, or act of aggression and shall make recommendations or decide what measures shall be taken in accordance with Articles 41 and 42, to maintain or restore international peace and security.

2. See the following applicable articles of the UN Charter which read:

Art. 2(4) All Members shall refrain in their international relations from the threat or use of force against the territorial integrity or political independence of any state, or in any other manner inconsistent with the purposes of the United Nations.

Art. 51 Nothing in the present Charter shall impair the inherent right of individual or collective self-defense if an armed attack occurs against a Member of the United Nations, until the Security Council has taken the measures necessary to maintain international peace and security.

See also articles 1(1) and 42 U.N. Charter as well as "Uniting for Peace," Resolution 377(v) of the General Assembly, 5 U.N. GAOR, Supp. 2(A/1775), pp. 10-12 (Nov. 3, 1950).

3. See C. Pompe, Aggressive War an International Crime 97 (1953); B. Röling, "The Question of Defining Aggression," Symbolae Verzijl 314 at 319 (1958).

4. See Q. Wright, "Subversive Intervention," 54 Am. J. Int. L. 521 at 529 (1960). Wright of course is of the opinion that such nonviolent acts should not be called aggression at all. Id.

5. See discourse of Cuban representative before Initiative Committee, Ninth International Conference of American States, Ministerio de Relaciones Exteriores, Bogotá, Colombia, Novena Conferencia Internacional Americana, Actas 6 Documentos, vol. 2, 347-48 (1953).

6. See infra p. 55. See also I. Brownlie, International Law and the Use of Force by States 364-65 (1963).

7. See infra pp. 90-92.

8. See infra pp. 83-89.

9. See Report by the Secretary General, 7 U.N. GAOR Annexes, Agenda Item 54, doc. A/2211, p. 17 at 72 (Oct. 3, 1952); M. McDougal and F. Feliciano, Law and Minimum World Public Order 190 (1961).

10. Id.

11. See H. Kelsen, "Collective Security under International Law," Naval War College International Law Studies 1954, 65 (1957); Pompe, supra note 3, at 53.

12. The fully sovereign state at international law is defined as one possessing the following qualifications: (1) a permanent population; (2) a defined territory; (3) government; and (4) capacity to enter into relations with other states. See International Conferences of American States 1933-1944, First Supp., p. 122 (1940).

13. Such international organizations are considered as international persons possessing certain international rights and being subjected to certain international duties. See Reparation for injuries suffered in the service of the United Nations, Advisory Opinion, I.C.J. Reports 1949, p. 144.

14. For example, the General Assembly found that Communist China had engaged in aggression by its hostilities directed against Korean and United Nations forces in Korea. See 5 U.N. GAOR, Supp. 20A, doc. A/1175/Add. 1, p. 1 (1951).

15. The General Assembly has condemned the Central People's Government of the People's Republic of China for aggression in Korea, although that government had not been recognized as the government of China by many nations. Id. See also Brownlie, supra note 6, at 379-80.

16. For discussion see H. Kelsen, The Law of the United Nations 59-60 (1950); A. Ross, The Constitution of the United Nations 43 (1950).

17. 12 U.N. GAOR, supp. 16, doc. A/3574 (1957).

18. Paragraph II of the Six Power Draft, Report of the Special Committee on the Question of Defining Aggression 24 February-3 April 1969, 24 U.N. GAOR, Supp. 20, doc. A/7620, p. 8 (1969).

19. A.V.W. Thomas and A. J. Thomas, Jr., The Organization of American States 340 (1963).

20. On insurgency and belligerency see id. at 340-41.

21. See, e.g., The Case of the Steamer Caroline, 2 J. B. Moore, A Digest of International Law sec. 217 (1906) which was concerned with a right of self-defense against

insurgents. For discussion see I C. Hyde, International Law Chiefly as Interpreted and Applied by the United States 239-44 (2nd rev. ed. 1947); C. Fenwick, International Law 274 (4th ed. 1965).

22. For example, see definitions in draft proposals as set forth in Report of the Special Committee on the Question of Defining Aggression, *supra* note 18, at 4-10.

23. For discussion of the varying limits as to the extent of the territorial sea, see M. McDougal and W. Burke, The Public Order of the Oceans, chap. 5 (1962); E. Jones, International Law: Its Application to the Mineral Resources of the Ocean 86-98 (unpublished thesis, Southern Methodist University School of Law 1970).

24. See C. Colombos, International Law of the Sea 88-89 (5th ed. 1962).

25. 1 L. Oppenheim, International Law 289-97 (8th ed., Lauterpacht, 1955).

26. Art. 2(4) UN Charter.

27. R. Alfaro, "Memorandum on the Question of Defining Aggression," 2 Y. B. Int'l L. Comm'n 36 (1951).

28. C. Waldock, "The Regulation of the Use of Force by Individual States in International Law," 81 Recueil des Cours 455 at 464-67; D. Bowett, Self-Defense in International Law 87 (1958) *et seq.*; A. Ross, A Textbook of International Law 244 (1947); G. Fitzmaurice, "The General Principles of International Law Considered from the Standpoint of the Rule of Law," 92 Recueil des Cours 5 at 173 (1957); Brownlie, *supra* note 6, at 289.

29. *Id.*

30. See, e.g., B. Supervielle, "Las Nuevas formas de Agresion," 11 Revista de la Facultad de Derecho y Ciencias Sociales (Uruguay 1960) 435, where at 446 he speaks of aggression as activity producing or propitiating a violation of rights and legitimate interests of a state or group of states. He adds that such activity must create a risk to peace and security.

31. See, e.g., D. Bowett, Self-Defense in International Law chap. II and in particular pp. 260-61.

32. See *supra* pp. 4-15.

33. *Id.* See also Pompe, *supra* note 3, at 49, 51, 57-58.

34. U.N. GAOR, 1968 Special Committee on the Question of Defining Aggression, Summary Records of the First to Twenty-Fourth Meetings, doc., A/AC. 134/SR. 1-24 (Sept. 30, 1968) at pp. 80-81.

35. See Alfaro, *supra* note 27, at 36, where he criticizes the word "unprovoked" as introducing into the determination of the aggressor the "vague, imprecise, and uncertain element of provocation."

36. See Thomas and Thomas, *supra* note 19, at 255-60 on the right of self-defense under the UN Charter and the Rio Treaty.

37. *Id.* at 257. Brownlie, *supra* note 6 points out at 227-28 and 426 that the doctrine of provocation is to be regarded as mainly political in nature.

38. See, e.g., Twelve Power Draft submitted in 1968, art. 4. 23 U.N. GAOR, Report of the Special Committee on the Question of Defining Aggression, Agenda Item 86, doc. A/7185/Rev. 1, p. 5.

39. *Id.*

40. J. Spiropoulos speaks of the necessity of an *animus aggresiones*. See 6 U.N. GAOR, Sixth Committee, 279th Meeting, para. 10, and 292nd Meeting, para. 9 (1952). See also G. Scelle, Memorandum on the question of the definition of aggression, submitted to the I.L.C. 2 Y. B. Int'l L. Comm'n 41-42 (1951).

41. 2 J. Stephen, History of the Criminal Law of England 110 (1883).

42. 1 F. Wharton, Criminal Law 192 (11th ed. 1912).

43. See Report of the Special Committee on the Question of Defining Aggression, *supra* note 18, at 27-28.

44. *Id.* at 28.

45. *Id.*

46. *Id.* at 19. For certain jurists maintaining that aggressive intent should not be part of the definition of aggression see Brownlie, *supra* note 6, at 377, n. 4. Brownlie himself would say the intention "is not a pre-condition for the existence of an unlawful

resort to force," but he would say that it is relevant in the determination of criminal responsibility. *Id.* at 377. See also Pompe, *supra* note 3, at 103, 114.

47. Report of the Special Committee on the Question of Defining Aggression, *supra* note 18, at 28.

48. *Id.* at 19.

49. See *supra*, chap. 2. For studies connecting aggression with the use of armed force see Q. Wright, The Role of International Law 59-60 (1961); P. Jessup, Rapporteur, Harvard Research Draft Convention on Rights and Duties of States in Case of Aggression, 33 Am. J. Int. L. Supp. 829 *et seq.* (1939); Röling, On Aggression, on International Criminal Law, on International Criminal Jurisdiction," 2 Nederlands Tijdschrift voor International Recht 167 at 170-71 (1955); Pompe, *supra* note 3, at 111, 113 (1953); H. J. Dupuy, "Aggression Indirecte et Intervention Sollicitée à propos de l'Affaire Libanaise," 5 Annuare Français de Droit International 460 (1959); G. Piotrowski, "Ou en sommes-nous sur le problème de l'agression?" 35 Revue de Droit International (Sottile) 178 (1957).

50. L.N.O.J., 20th Year, No. 11-12 (Part II), 107th Sess. of the Council, doc. A. 46. 1939, VII, p. 540.

51. Art. 6(a), Charter of the International Military Tribunal as contained in Report of Robert H. Jackson, United States Representative to the International Conference on Military Trials, Dept. State Pub. 3080, p. 423 (1949).

52. See 1 Trial of the Major War Criminals before the International Military Tribunal, Nuremberg, 14 December 1945-1 October 1946, pp. 192-94, wherein the seizure of Austria is so described. See Pompe, *supra* note 3, at 21-22, and Brownlie, *supra* note 6, at 211.

53. For summary of UN action in the Korean affair as to aggression see Report by the Secretary General, *supra* note 9, at 45-46.

54. Resolution 498V, 5 U.N. GAOR, Supp. 20A, doc. A/1175/Add. 1, p. 1 (1951).

55. For various views see Report by the Secretary General, *supra* note 9, at 68 *et seq.*; Pompe, *supra* note 3, at 112-13, Brownlie, *supra* note 6, at 364-65; Q. Wright, "The Prevention of Aggression," 50 Am. J. Int. L. 514 at 526 (1956). See also for discussion, Röling, *supra* note 49, at 175.

56. Wright, *id* at 526.

57. *Id.* at 527-29; see also Q. Wright, "Subversive Intervention," 54 Am. J. Int. L. 521 at 529 (1960).

58. L. Sohn, "The Definition of Aggression," 45 Va. L. Rev. 697 at 701 (1959).

59. "Uniting for Peace," Resolution 377A(V), 5 U.N. GAOR, Supp. 20, doc. A/1775, pp. 10-12 (1950).

60. See Report by Secretary General, *supra* note 9, at 69 *et seq.*

61. Pompe, *supra* note 3, 97.

62. *Id.* at 104.

63. *Id.* at 111.

64. *Id.* at 69-70; D. Bowett, *supra* note 28, at chap. XI. On self-defense and aggression see G. Scelle, "L'Agression et la Légitime Défense dans les Rapports Internationaux." 10 L'Espirit International 372 (1936).

65. Art. 2(4) UN Charter.

66. L. Goodrich and E. Hambro, Charter of the United Nations 104 (Rev. ed. 1949). See also M. Singh, "The Right of Self-Defense in Relation to the Use of Nuclear Weapons," 5 Indian Y. B. Int'l Affairs 3 at 24 (1956).

67. 2 L. Oppenheim, International Law 156 (Lauterpacht 7th ed. 1952).

68. See *infra*, chap. 4 on subversion and ideological aggression in particular.

69. See Thomas and Thomas, *supra* note 19, at 252, 267-68.

70. Art. 39.

71. See "Uniting for Peace," *supra* note 59.

72. This theory is espoused by Bowett, *supra* note 64, at 251-56.

73. 2 Oppenheim, *supra* note 67, at 160, 163; H. Kelsen, Law of the United Nations 724 *et seq.* (1950).

74. The confusion that can and has come about from attempting to define aggression differently for different purposes is demonstrated by the viewpoint of various authors. Bowett, for example, would see some reason for excluding acts not involving the use of force from a definition of aggression for purposes of collective action, for such nonviolent acts are not so likely to jeopardize international peace and security. On the other hand, any illegal act—forceful or not—which endangers the security of a state would give rise to the right of self-defense. Bowett, *supra* note 64, at 260-61. Pompe, on the other hand, would seem to think that the organs of collective security can react against aggressive acts regardless of whether the acts involve the use of force, but that self-defense is limited to the use of force. Pompe, *supra* note 3, at 99-100.

75. Article 39 of the UN Charter authorizes the Security Council to decide what measures are necessary for the maintenance or restoration of international peace. Article 42 speaks of measures involving military force which the Security Council may order if the lesser measures of an economic or diplomatic nature, which may be decided upon by the Security Council under Article 41, prove inadequate. Uniting for Peace permits the General Assembly to recommend any appropriate collective measures, although armed force as a collective measure is reserved for a breach of the peace or an act of aggression. See note 59 *supra.*

76. On the interrelation of self-discipline and aggression see Pompe, *supra* note 3, at 48 and 102 *et seq.* See also Bowett, *supra* note 64, at 249-50; G. Fitzmaurice, "The Definition of Aggression," 1 Int. & Comp. L.Q. 137 (1952).

77. The right has never been seriously questioned. See, for example, J. Brierly, the Law of Nations 253 (2d ed. 1938); H. Kelsen, Principles of International Law 60-61 (1952); 1 C. Hyde, International Law Chiefly as Interpreted and Applied by the United States, sec. 70 (2d ed. 1947).

78. A. V. W. Thomas and A. J. Thomas, Jr., Non-Intervention: The Law and Its Import in the Americas 79 *et seq.* (1956).

79. See, for example, Kelsen, *supra* note 77, at 792; J. Kunz, "Individual and Collective Self-Defense in Article 51 of the Charter of the United Nations," 41 Am. J. Int. L. 872 (1947); A. Ross, A Textbook of International Law 244 (1947).

80. See, for example, Bowett, *supra* note 64, chap. I; B. Cheng, General Principles of International Law as Applied by International Courts and Tribunals 94 *et seq.* (1953); 1 Hyde, *supra* note 77, sec. 70 (1947); 1 G. Schwarzenberger, A Manual of International Law 172-73 (4th ed. 1960).

81. The essential rights of a state the violation of which would justify self-defense are, according to Bowett, the following: the right of territorial integrity, the right of political independence, the right of protection of nationals, and certain economic rights. Bowett, *id.* Part I and as summed up in the conclusion at p. 270.

82. Bowett, *id.* at 23-25.

83. *Supra* note 81.

84. Bowett, *id.* at 3-4.

85. For example, Kelsen and Beckett are of the opinion that the right of self-defense under the Charter is limited to action after an armed attack has occurred. W. Beckett, The North Atlantic Treaty 13 (1950); Kelsen, *supra* note 16, at 791 *et seq.* Kunz also takes this position, Kunz, *supra* note 79.

86. See Bowett, *supra* note 64, chaps. IX and X; J. Stone, Aggression and World Order chap. 5 (1958).

87. Bowett, *id.* at 188.

88. *Id.* at 185 and 186. Stone reaches a similar view in his interpretation of article 2(4) and other articles of the UN Charter. Stone, *supra* note 86, at 94-97. Rights of territorial integrity and political independence are not absolute, but relative; and when a state violates essential legal rights of another, it can hardly claim absolute inviolability of its own political independence and territorial integrity from a legitimate action of self-defense by the wronged state to protect its own security, i.e., its right of political independence and territorial integrity, in the absence of other means of protection. Moreover, a defense by the state of its legitimate interests can hardly be inconsistent

with the purposes of the United Nations where that or other international organization fails to achieve the "purposes." See Bowett, *id.*

89. Cheng, *supra* note 80, at 101.

90. M. McDougal and F. Feliciano, "Legal Regulation of Resort to International Coercion, Aggression and Self-Defense in Policy Perspective," 68 Yale L. J. 1057 at 1120 (1959).

91. Bowett, *supra* note 64, at 24.

92. *Id.* at 110.

93. United Kingdom comment on article 4 of the Draft Declaration on the Rights and Duties of States as quoted in Bowett, *id.*

94. See Bowett, *id.* at 50. The extent of the duties of a state to suppress activities detrimental to another state and its political independence may also be uncertain. See M. Garcia Mora, "International Responsibility for Subversive Activities and Hostile Propaganda by Private Persons against Foreign States," 35 Ind. L. J. 306 (1959-60).

95. P.A.U., Final Act Ninth Meeting of Consultation of Ministers of Foreign Affairs, Washington, D. C., July 21-26, 1964.

96. McDougal and Feliciano, *supra* note 90, at 1119.

97. *Id.*

98. *Id.* at 1120.

99. See *supra* pp. 54-57.

100. See M. McDougal, "Peace and War: Factual Continuum with Multiple Legal Consequences," 49 Am. J. Int. L. 63 (1955). He points out that a wide range of coercion ranging from the secret use of armed force to unarmed methods such as economic or ideological coercion are today utilized by states against other states. With states increasingly resorting to methods not necessarily involving a direct use of armed force, there has come about a demand that the rules of international law be updated, and that an intermediate status between war and peace be recognized in order to give greater precision to the rights and duties of states. See G. Schwarzenberger, "*Jus Paci ac Belli*," 37 Am. J. Int. L. 474 (1943); G. Schwarzenberger, Power Politics 191 (3rd ed. 1964); F. Grob, The Relativity of War and Peace 3 (1949); P. Jessup, "Should International Law Recognize an Intermediate Status between Peace and War?" 48 Am. J. Int. L. 98 (1954).

101. See McDougal and Feliciano, *supra* note 9, at 190; Pompe, *supra* note 3, at 52, 111. Brownlie, *supra* note 6, at 369-72 (1963); Kelsen, *supra* note 11, at 64.

102. See E. Aroneanu, La Définition de l'Agression 90 (1958).

103. *Id.*

104. G. Schwarzenberger, Frontiers of International Law 155 (1962).

105. Webster's Collegiate Dictionary (5th ed. 1936).

106. Kelsen, *supra* note 11, at 64; Pompe, *supra* note 3, at 111.

107. Draft proposal of the Soviet Union presented to the 1969 session of the Special Committee on the Question of Defining Aggression as contained in the committee's report *supra* note 18, at 5.

108. For discussion see *supra* pp. 19-20.

109. As set forth in the Report of the Secretary General, *supra* note 9, at 35.

110. Kelsen, *supra* note 11, at 64.

111. On the broader notion of indirect aggression see Report by the Secretary General, *supra* note 9, at 72 *et seq.*

112. Union of Soviet Socialist Republics: draft resolution, 9 U.N. GAOR, Ad Hoc Political Committee Annexes, Agenda Item 51, Doc. A/C.6/L.332/Rev. 1, pp. 6-7 (1954).

113. On indirect aggression in this context see B. Supervielle, *supra* note 30, at 466; Aroneanu, *supra* note 102, at 75-76. See also the Inter-American Treaty of Reciprocal Assistance (Rio Treaty) which in Article 3 speaks of individual and collective measures in an exercise of the right of collective self-defense and which in Article 6 speaks of the employment of such measures against an act of aggression which is not armed attack. Aggression must therefore include acts not involving the use of armed force.

CHAPTER FOUR

1. See statements of intervention as indirect aggression set forth in Report by the Secretary General, "Question of the Definition of Aggression," 7 U.N. GAOR, Annexes, Agenda Item 54, Doc. A/2211, p. 73 (1952).

2. On the principle of non-intervention see A.V.W. Thomas and A. J. Thomas, Jr., Non-Intervention: The Law and Its Import in the Americas (1956).

3. Art. 5, Charter of the OAS as contained in Ninth International Conference of American States, Bogota, Colombia, March 30-May 2, 1948, Report of the Delegation of the U.S.A., p. 168-86 (1948).

4. Art. 16, *id.*

5. Text of Resolution, U.N. doc. A/Res/2131 (xx); adopted in plenary session of the General Assembly on December 21, 1965, by a vote of 109 to 0, with 1 abstention. As set forth in 54 Dept. State Bull. 128-29 (1966).

6. *Id.*

7. See Thomas and Thomas, *supra* note 2, at 74-78.

8. P.A.U., Applications of the Inter-American Treaty of Reciprocal Assistance 1948-1956, p. 126 (1957).

9. 3 Annals of the OAS 10-11 (1951).

10. Haedrich gives a discussion of the various forms of interventionary acts which reads much like a description of aggressive acts. Intervention by use of arms and less aggravating encroachments are distinguished. Both forms may be applied in indirect or direct coercion. Differing techniques of intervention are mentioned such as military, economic, financial, or diplomatic means of coercion. The incitement or support of revolutionary movements in other states is described as intervention. H. Haedrich, "Intervention," as set forth in 2 Strupp-Schlochauer, Woerterbuch des Voelkerrechts 146 (1960). For discussion of various forms of intervention see also Thomas and Thomas, *supra* note 2, Bk III.

11. For definition and discussion of the concept, "intervention," see Thomas and Thomas, *id.* at 71.

12. *Id.*

13. See *supra* pp. 50-51.

14. *Id.*

15. Intervention may be legal or illegal. Collective measures of the international community, interventionary acts taken in self-defense, and reprisals for violations of international legal duties are recognized by international law as legal. Thomas and Thomas, *supra* note 2, at 74 *et seq.*

16. See *supra* pp. 26, 28, 33, 34, 39, 42.

17. *Id.*

18. As early as the eighteenth century Vattel roundly condemned nations for intermeddling in the internal affairs of neighboring states, declaring: "Each ought to render to the other what belongs to them, to respect their rights, and to leave them in the peaceable enjoyment of them." E. de Vattel, The Law of Nations, Bk. II, chap. 5, sec. 64 (Chitty ed. 1876).

19. See, e.g., the 1928 Havana Convention on Duties and Rights of States in the Event of Civil Strife which made many of these activities illegal. P.A.U., Treaties and Conventions Signed at the Sixth International Conference of American States, Havana, Cuba, January 16-February 20, 1928, pp. 19-20 (1950). For discussions of authors see H. Wehberg, "La Guerre Civile et le Droit International," 63 Recueil des Cours 7 (1938); L. Podesta Costa, Ensayo Sobre las Luchas Civiles y el Derecho Internacional (1926).

20. See C. De Visscher, Theory and Reality in Public International Law 294 (1957); J. Herz, International Politics in the Atomic Age 168 (1959).

21. F. Greene, Dynamics of International Relations: Power, Security and Order 640 (1964).

22. As quoted by "A" "The Ideological War," 4 Australian Outlook 222 at 227 (1950).

23. "In countries which are unable to achieve the contentment of their middle and working classes with the means at the disposal of democratic governments, social discontent and Communism form formidable fifth columns of the Soviet Union." G. Schwarzenberger, Power Politics 123-24 (2d ed. 1951).

24. For a short discussion of some of the techniques used in subversive activities see "Cuba as a Base for Subversion in America," A Study Presented to the Subcommittee to Investigate the Administration of the Internal Security Act and Other Internal Security Laws of the Committee on the Judiciary, U.S. Senate, 88th Cong. 1st Sess. pp. 4-6 (1963).

25. In addition those engaged in subversive activities also take "advantage of 'useful fools,' working freely through them. . . ." *Id*. at 5.

The Communists prefer to work with sympathizers whose formal organization tie-in with the Party either does not exist or could never be established . . . A professor who—without being a communist party member—stands up for the interests of the Soviet Union is more valuable than a hundred men with a membership-book. The writer who—being no party member—stands up for the Soviet Union, the trade union leader who defends the international politics of the Soviet Union, is more valuable than a thousand party members.

W. Kintner and J. Kornfeder, The New Frontier of War; Political Warfare, Present and Future 80 (1962).

26. See L. Hart, The Strategy of Indirect Approach 155 (1946).

27. General MacArthur in a statement on "Military Situation in the Far East" declared:

They practice the tremendous psychological factors of propaganda, of creating confusion, of bewilderment, of belittling and assassinating characters of the people who are opposed to them, of all the methods of the fifth column, which have so undermined the confidence of free peoples in their own institutions—those things are raging every day in almost every country of the world. They have nothing to do with military force, but they are allied with it.

Pt. I, Hearings before the Committee on Armed Services and the Committee on Foreign Relations, U.S. Senate, 82nd Cong., 1st Sess., p. 277 (1951).

28. T. Wyckoff, "War by Subversion," 59 South Atlantic Q. 36 (1960).

29. "How do we define diplomacy? The classic Western definition assumes a common field of interest between sovereign governments. It is the job of the diplomat to find this common ground and to build on it. But there is a fundamental difference between Soviet diplomacy and that of the free world. Soviet diplomacy is predicated upon an assumption that there are no enduring common interests between the Soviet Union and the so-called capitalist countries. The Soviet goal is to destroy the capitalist world. The Soviet diplomat is, therefore, part of a world-wide conspiratorial and ideological scheme. Within his embassy he is the instrument of such non-diplomatic agencies as the secret police and the Communist party." Statement of Ray Thurston in discussion on paper of C. E. Black, "The Role of Diplomacy in Soviet Imperialism," in The Threat of Soviet Imperialism edited by C. G. Haines at p. 117 (1954).

30. C. Pompe, Aggressive War an International Crime 52 (1953).

31. *Id*. See also Report by the Secretary General, *supra* note 1, at 72-73.

32. *Id*.

33. Subversion designates all illegal activities, whether direct or indirect, overt or covert, conducted under the auspices of the authorities of a state and calculated to overthrow the existing government or public order of another state. External affairs as well as internal affairs are part of the public order of a state. States possess not only internal but also external self-determination.

34. See Report by the Secretary General, *supra* note 1, at 72.

35. OAS Dept. Legal Affairs, Background Memorandum on the Convocation of the Meeting, Eighth Meeting of Consultation of Ministers of Foreign Affairs Serving

as Organ of Consultation in the Application of the Inter-American Treaty of Reciprocal Assistance, Punta del Este, Uruguay, January, 1962, p. 3, OEA Off. Rec., OEA/Ser.F/11.8; See also Art. 2, Statutes of the Special Consultative Committee on Security, Official Records OAS, OEA/Ser.1/X/i. (1963).

36. See, e.g., the remarks of the representative of Ghana, *supra* p. 38.

37. See text of the Charter in 48 Am. J. Int. L. 873 *et seq.* (1964).

38. *Id.*

39. See C. Sanger, "Toward Unity in Africa," 42 Foreign Affairs 296 at 277-78 (Jan. 1964).

40. 12 U. N. GAOR, 1st Comm., 913th meeting, p. 256 (Nov. 27, 1957).

41. *Id.*

42. *Id.*

43. *Id.*

44. *Id.* 916th meeting, p. 274 (Dec. 2, 1957).

45. *Id.*

46. Drafts are contained in Report of the Special Committee on the Question of Defining Aggression, 23 U. N. GAOR, Agenda item 86, doc. A/7185/Rev. L (1967) and in Report of the Special Committee on the Question of Defining Aggression 24 February - 3 April 1969, 24 U. N. GAOR, Supp. No. 20, doc. A/7620.

47. Art. 6 of the draft, 1969 Report, *id.* at 6.

48. *Id.*

49. This falls within the sovereignty of the state. For discussion see 1 L. Oppenheim, International Law 286-97 (8th ed. Lauterpacht, 1955).

50. See A.V.W. Thomas and A. J. Thomas, Jr., The Organization of American States, chap. 18 (1963).

51. See Background Memorandum, *supra* note 35, at 12, and P.A.U., Report on the Third Meeting of Ministers of Foreign Affairs of the American Republics, Rio de Janeiro, Jan. 15-28, 1942, Resolution XVII (Cong. and Conf. Series No. 32, 1940). See also P.A.U., Strengthening of Internal Security; Report prepared in compliance with Resolution of Foreign Affairs, Washington, D.C., March 26-April 7, 1951, pp. 19, 26, 37 (1953).

52. Resolution XCII, Tenth Inter-American Conference, Caracas, Venezuela, March 1-28, 1954, Report of the Delegation of the U.S.A. (Dept. State Pub. 5692, Int. Org. and Conf. Series II, American Republics 14, 1955).

53. Art. 2, Statutes of the Special Consultative Committee on Security, Official Records OAS, OEA/Ser. L/X/i. (1963).

54. Report of the Special Consultative Committee on Security, OEA/Ser. L/X/ii.4, Oct. 18, 1963.

55. Ninth Meeting of Consultation of Ministers of Foreign Affairs, Washington, D.C., as set forth in P.A.U., Tratado Interamericana de Asistencia Reciprocal Aplicaciones, vol. 2, 1960-1964, 183 *et seq.* (1964).

56. Res. 290, "Essentials for Peace," 4 U.N. GAOR, doc. A/1251 (1949).

57. "Report by the Commission of Investigation Concerning Greek Frontier Incidents," 5 U.N. SCOR, 2d yr. doc. S. 360, Rev. 9, Spec. Supp. No. 2, Vol. 1, Part IV, chap. 1, p. 154 (July 28, 1950).

58. Union of Soviet Socialist Republics: draft resolution, 9 U.N. GAOR, Ad Hoc Political Committee Annexes, Agenda item 51, doc. A/C.6/L. 332/Rev. 1, pp. 6-7 (1954).

59. See Wyckoff, *supra* note 28, at 37. For these drafts see *supra* note 46.

60. Statement by Mr. Röling of the Netherlands. 9 U.N. GAOR, 410th Meeting of the Sixth Committee, para. 37 (1954).

61. De Visscher, *supra* note 20, at 295.

62. See note 58, *supra.*

63. Art. C of Soviet draft, Report of Special Committee 1969, *supra* note 46.

64. For summary of the OAS and subversion see Inter-American Institute of International Legal Studies, The Inter-American System 113-19 (1966).

65. 2 P.A.U., Applications of the Inter-American Treaty of Reciprocal Assistance 1960-1964, 181, 201 (1964).

66. *Id.*

67. *Id.* at 186.

68. See 1 L. Oppenheim, International Law, secs. 123-28 (8th ed. Lauterpacht, 1955).

69. See Report by the Secretary General, *supra* note 1, at 72-73.

70. H. Lasswell, "Psychology of Propaganda," Proceedings Sixth Conference Teachers of International Law 52 (1938).

71. On propaganda at international law see Lasswell, *id.*; J. Whitton, "Propaganda and International Law," 72 Recueil des Cours 545 (1958); L. Preuss, "International Responsibility for Hostile Propaganda against Foreign States," 28 Am. J. Int. L. 649 (1934).

72. J. Whitton and A. Larson, Propaganda: Towards Disarmament in the War of Words 56 (1963).

73. League of Nations, IX Disarmament Conference 1935, Doc. 1-4, p. 702.

74. Whitton and Larson, *supra* note 72, at 83.

75. *Id.* at 95.

76. *Id.* at 104.

77. "The right of respect manifests itself in the requirement that neither the heads of sovereign states nor their diplomatic representatives or emblems shall be injured or insulted." C. Eagleton, International Government 86 (3rd ed. 1957).

78. 1 A. McNair, International Law Opinions 12 (1956).

79. Cuba, p. 29 Dept. State Publications 7171, Inter-American Series 66 (1961).

80. 1958 Y.B.U.N. 36 (1960).

81. *Id.* at 50.

82. 1959 Y.B.U.N. 62.

83. *Id.* at 65-66.

84. P.A.U., 1 Inter-American Treaty of Reciprocal Assistance Applications, 1948-1959, p. 69 (1964).

85. *Id.* at 70.

86. The case was turned over to the Inter-American Peace Committee which obtained the signatures of both nations on a document in which they agreed not to tolerate in their territories the activities of any persons or groups, national or foreign, that have as their object the disturbance of domestic peace of either nation. 1 Annals of the OAS 325 (1949).

87. P.A.U., Report of the Inter-American Peace Committee to the Eighth Meeting of Consultation of Ministers of Foreign Affairs 1962, p. 22 (OEA/Ser.L./III, CIP/1/62, 1962).

88. *Id.* at 36.

89. P.A.U., 2 Inter-American Treaty of Reciprocal Assistance Applications 1960-1964, p. 75 (1964).

90. *Id.* at 70.

91. P.A.U., Report of the Special Consultative Committee on Security on the Work Done during Its Fifth Regular Meeting, October 18 to November 10, 1965, 6 (OEA/Ser.L/X/II.10, Nov. 10, 1965).

92. P.A.U., *supra* note 89, at 181.

93. *Id.* at 197.

94. *Id.* at 185.

95. *Id.* at 186.

96. N.Y. Times, March 8, 1966.

97. Set out in Am. Soc. Int. L., 5 International Legal Materials: Current Documents, p. 138 (Jan., 1966).

98. See *supra* p. 63.

99. See *supra* pp. 65-68. The Soviet enumerative definition of 1954 lists as acts of ideological aggression the encouragement of war propaganda, the encouragement of propaganda in favor of using atomic, bacterial, chemical, and other weapons of mass

THE CONCEPT OF AGGRESSION IN INTERNATIONAL LAW

destruction, the promotion of the propagation of fascist-nazi views, of racial and national exclusiveness, and of hatred and contempt for other peoples. These acts would not seem to exhaust all conduct falling within the field of ideological aggression. Moreover, the listed acts do not seem to be in and of themselves aggression. For the Soviet definition see note 58, *supra.*

100. E. de Vattel, The Law of Nations or the Principles of Natural Law Applied to the Conduct and to the Affairs of Nations and of Sovereigns (C. Fenwick's Translation of the Edition of 1758), Book II, chap. 6, sec. 72.

101. See 3 C. Calvo, Le Droit International Theorique et Pratique, Sec. 1298 (5th ed. 1896); 1 P. Pradier-Fodere, Traite de Droit International Public Europeen et Americain, Sec. 260 (1885); 1 J. de Louter, Le Droit International Public Positif 248 (1920).

102. See, e.g., S. Biro, "International Aspects of Radio Control," 2 J. of Radio Law 45 (1932).

103. "Such acts are considered so heinous that even in time of war they are held to constitute a violation of international law." Whitton and Larson, *supra* note 72, at 141.

104. As contained in 5 M. Whiteman, Digest of International Law 831 (1965).

105. *Id.* at 832.

106. On the Grau Doctrine see L. Guillen Atienza, El Principio Internacional de no Intervencion y las Doctrinas Americanas chap. 6 (1949); M. Campa, La Doctrina Grau y la Agresión Económica, 54 Revista de Derecho Internacional 150 (1948).

107. For text of the charter see *supra* note 3.

108. See L. Podesta Costa, Manual de Derecho Internacional Público 229 (2d ed. 1947); E. Milhaud, L'organization économique de la paix, 15 Recueil des Cours 281 (1926); W. Rappard, Le nationalisme économique et la Société des Nations, 61 Recueil des Cours 103 (1937).

109. Arts. 15 and 16 of the Charter of the OAS prohibit economic intervention, as does the General Assembly's 1965 non-intervention resolution. The resolution is cited *supra* note 5.

110. *Id.*

111. See Thomas and Thomas, *supra* note 2, at 410-11.

112. See Report by the Secretary General, *supra* note 1, at 74.

113. B. Supervielle, "Las Nuevas Formas de Agresión," 11 Revista de la Facultad de Derecho y Ciencias Sociales (Uruguay) 510 (1960).

114. Draft resolution cited *supra* note 58.

115. Report of the Special Committee on the Question of Defining Aggression, at 9-10, 9 U.N. GAOR, Supp. No. 11, doc. A/2638, pp. 9-10 (1953).

INDEX

Abstract definition, 6, 7, 8, 9, 10, 29

Afghanistan, 19

Africa, 9

Aggredior, 14

Aggression: atomic, biological, and chemical weapons, 42; absence of definition, 10; accusations of, 3, 4, 37; acts called, 19, 29, 42, 45-47, 54, 77-78, 82-83; against people, 50; and aggressive intent, 43, 50-54; armed, 23, 32, 34-35, 40, 45, 49, 51, 54-65, 80, 91-92; and belligerency, 49; case against defining, 4-8; case for defining, 4, 8-12; and cease-fire, 22; and civil strife, 23, 31, 32, 42; and Chaco War, 20; and colonialism, 45; and collective security, 11, 15, 20, 45, 51-52, 55, 57-58, 83; and common law, 4; and Communist Chinese, 44; compromise definition of, 4; and confiscation, 7; and *de facto* governments, 47-49; and defense of nationals abroad, 50; desirability of ambiguity, 5; direct and indirect, 29, 46, 47, 58, 65-68, 80; and Draft Code of Offenses against Peace and Security, 23-28, 89; early meanings of, 14-16, 69; elements of, 5, 21, 45, 46, 47, 50, 52; external, 16; first attack as, 15, 19, 21, 43, 44, 51, 66; illegal, 14, 23, 45, 72; and insurgency, 49; intent and, 50-54; internal, 75-76, 78; as international crime, 17, 23, 39; and international peace, 3, 31, 45, 56-65; intervention and, 21, 69-72; and League of Nations, 16-21; legal, 14, 43; legal consequences of, 43, 45; legal defense for, 5, 60; legal elements of, 5, 56-65; and Manchuria, 20; natural notions of, 10-11; necessity of defense, 56-57; need to define, 12, 22, 28-29; nonmilitary, 26, 46, 83, 86; by nonstate entities, 39, 43, 47; nonofficial definitions, 6, 10; and Nuremberg, 20, 25, 54; and Peace through Deeds Resolution, 23; political, 82-83, 86; as political concept, 12; possible definitional loopholes, 9; preventive, 3; and private criminal law, 14; by proxy, 65-66, 68; and provocation, 41, 51, 52;

publicists views on defining, 7-9; treaties relating to, 12, 13, 15, 17, 18, 19; types of definitions, 6-10; unarmed coercion as, 31, 40; and U.N. Charter, 45, 48, 54-65; U.N. debates on, 21-44; value of definition, 11; violation of international law as, 47, 57-59; Western views on, 9. *See also* Armed force, Economic aggression, Ideological aggression, Indirect aggression, Subversion

Aggressive intent, 43, 50-54

Aggressive war: and Bustamante, 14; and defensive alliances, 15; and defensive war, 22; as crime, 18, 20, 54-55; and Covenant of League of Nations, 17; just and unjust, 15, 16; illegality of, 15-16, 54-55; and Kellogg-Briand Pact, 18; and Korea, 55; and Suarez, 14-15; and Vattel, 15

Aggressors: and definition of aggression, 4; colonial powers as, 77-78; nonstate entities as, 39, 43, 47; states as, 47; stigmatization of, 4, 5; through indirect action, 65-69

Alessandri, A., 85

Alfaro, R., 24; on defining aggression, 9

Algerian War, 76-77

Annexation of territory: illegality of, 25, 54

Arab states: accused of aggression, 3; and Algerian War, 76-77

Armed bands: aid to, 21, 42, 65-67, 72-73; and aggression, 19, 24, 65-68; encouragement of, 47, 66-67; and subversion, 35, 37, 66-67, 81-82; support of, 19, 22, 25, 27, 31, 67

Armed force, 21, 24, 34, 46; as aggression, 19, 23, 25, 29-30, 43, 54-65; direct use of, 45, 62-63, 65; direct or indirect, 39, 65-68; illegal use of, 30, 57-63; and indirect aggression, 46, 56-57, 66, 67; indirect use of, 45; insignificant use of, 30, 53; and intervention, 71; preparation for, 25; in self-defense, 23, 24-25, 30, 31, 39, 54-65, 91; U.N. Charter on, 29-30, 45, 48, 54-65, 68; unprovoked use of, 41, 51, 52; use of, 31, 54-65

Arms limitation, 25
Asia, 9
Assembly of League of Nations, 17, 54
Atomic, biological, and chemical weapons: and aggression, 42; propaganda for, 33
Australia, 40
Austria's Anschluss, 46

Baltic States: and aggression, 3
Bandung Conference, 77
Belligerency: and aggression, 49
Betancourt, R., 85
Blockage, 18, 19, 33, 54, 91-92
Bolivia, 20, 21, 33, 91
Bowett, D., 64
Boycotts: and economic aggression, 91
Breach of peace, 21-22; and indirect aggression, 31; and U.N. Charter, 30
Brierly, J., 5
Bustamante, A., 14
Byelorussia, 48

Canada, 40
Castro, F., 79
Cease-fire and aggression, 22-23
Central Europe, 18-19
Centralized law enforcement: and international law, 61-62
Chaco War, 20
Charter of United Nations: See United Nations Charter
China, 33, 34, 55
Civil strife: and aggression, 23, 31, 32, 42; ambiguity of, 28; and economic aggression, 90; fomenting of, 23, 24, 25, 27-28, 67; and foreign interference, 56, 70; and indirect aggression, 67; and intervention, 70; legality of, 78; promotion of, 67; and subversion, 80-81; and subversive propaganda, 84-85
Citizenship: as element of aggression, 50
Codification, 5
Coercion: economic, 26, 57, 69, 91-92; intensity of, 22, 64-65; and propaganda, 75; psychological, 57; and subversion, 74, unarmed, 30
Collective security: and aggression, 11, 20, 56-65; and intervention, 70-71; and subversion, 75; and unprovoked armed attack, 51-52, 57-59
Collective self-defense. See Self-defense
Colonialism: as aggression, 77-78; and subversion, 76-77
Common law, 4
Communism: and inter-American system, 26, 86-87

Compromise: and definition of aggression, 9
Conference for the Reduction and Limitation of Armaments (1933), 19
Confiscation: and aggression, 7
Conspiracies: and subversion, 73-74
Constitutional law, 5-6, 10
Cordova, E., 26
Council of League of Nations, 16
Covenant of League of Nations, 16-17, 54
Crime, 8, 9
Crimes: against peace, 23, 54-55; international, 23-24
Criminality, 8
Cuba, 3, 24; and subversion, 79-80, 82-83, 85-89
Cultural aggression, 29, 47
Cyprus, 43
Czechoslovakia, 3, 46

Declaration of war: as aggression, 19, 21
Definition of aggression: case against, 4-6; case for, 8-12; effect of, 12-13; function of, 58-59; and purpose to be put to, 59-60; and sanctions, 12, 57-59; search for, 14-44; shortcomings of, 12; Soviet versions of, 8-9, 19-20, 32-33, 40, 67-68; in times of crisis, 12-13; types of, 6-8
Dependent people: and liberation movements, 77-78
Determination of aggression: by U.N., 39, 57-59, 60-65
Developing nations: political and economic integrity of, 9
Diplomacy: and subversion, 74-75; traditional, 75
Diplomatic relations, 18; and Cuba, 79-80, 82-83, 85-89
Disarmament, 18
Disarmament Conference of 1932-33, 66
Disputes: settlement of, 16, 17; and threat to peace, 31
Dominican Republic, 3, 86
Draft Code of Offenses against Peace and Security, 23-28, 89
Dumbarton Oaks Conference, 21
Duties of states: and aggression, 22

Economic aggression, 9, 24, 26, 29, 33, 34-35, 39, 40-41, 45, 46, 52, 64-68, 90-92; armed, 91-92; blockade as, 33, 90-92; and civil war, 32; Doctrina Grau on, 90; effects of, 90; illegality of, 92; as indirect aggression, 31, 32, 33; and international peace, 92; and intervention, 69, 92; methods of, 90-91; OAS